SHOW UP to RISE!

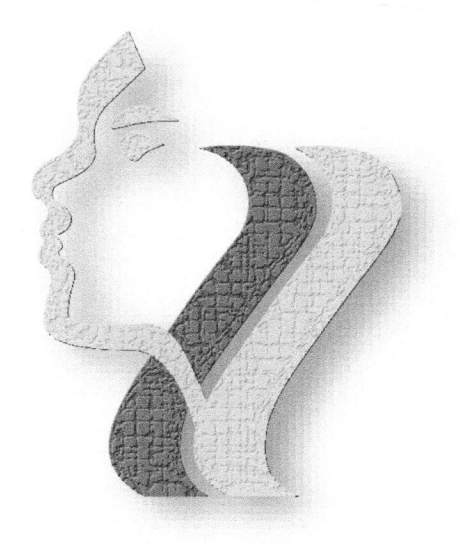

DR. MADELINE ANN LEWIS

A Successful Mindset
YOUR MINDSET IS YOUR SUPERPOWER OWN IT AND SOAR!

YOUR MINDSET IS YOUR SUPERPOWER OWN IT AND SOAR!

SHOW UP TO RISE UP!

DR. MADELINE ANN LEWIS

Copyright © 2024 by DR. MADELINE ANN LEWIS
All rights reserved. This book or any portion thereof may not be reproduced or used in any manner without the author's express written permission except for using brief quotations in a book review.

Disclaimer: The information contained in this book is based on the author's journey and experiences. Although the author and publisher have made every effort to ensure the accuracy and completeness of the information at the time of publication, they do not assume and hereby disclaim any liability to any party for any loss, damage, or disruption caused by errors or omissions, whether such errors or omissions result from negligence, accident, or any other cause. The content is provided for informational purposes only and should not be considered professional advice. Readers are encouraged to consult with a qualified professional before making any decisions based on the information provided in this book.

ISBN: 9798344592350

YOUR MINDSET IS YOUR SUPERPOWER OWN IT AND SOAR!

Show Up to RISE UP!

DR. MADELINE ANN LEWIS

DEDICATION

This book is dedicated to my mother, Mrs. Lilly G. Lewis, a woman of tremendous strength and courage and a significant influence and role model. She raised me to believe that anything I set out to do was possible. Her love, encouragement, and discipline made me a woman. She taught me how to be strong and gentle, and her prayers carried me from one side of this country to the other. She firmly believed that you always share your knowledge with those who need help or guidance. She also thought you should pull someone up when you get to the top.

Mom, I thank you for passing on your strength, courage, kind heart, and strong will, which gave me the perseverance to pursue my dreams. I owe all that I am and all that I ever hoped to be to you. The values you taught me, the care you gave me, and the wonderful love you showed me have enriched my life in more ways than I can count.

Mom, thanks for always being there.
You will always be in my heart.

Dr. Madeline Ann Lewis

Show Up to RISE UP!

DR. MADELINE ANN LEWIS

SHOW UP to RISE UP!

DR. MADELINE ANN LEWIS
BEST-SELLING VISIONARY AUTHOR

YOUR MINDSET IS YOUR SUPERPOWER OWN IT AND SOAR!

SHOW UP TO RISE UP!

DR. MADELINE ANN LEWIS

CONTENTS

Foreword 1
Acknowledgement 3
Introduction 6
A Personal Note! This Is YOUR TIME! 9
What Does Success Mean to You? 11
Harnessing the Power of Positive Thinking 25
Why Are Goals Important? 38
The Key to Professional and Personal Growth 50
The Secret Ingredients for Success 62
In Which Direction Art You Headed and Where You Will End Up? 73
Perseverance, Determination, and Belief in Yourself 79
Take Responsibilty for Your Life 86
Stop Blaming Others 94
Find Your Authentic Voice 99
Knowledge is Power: Do You Have the Power? 107
Those Shoes Are Made for Walking, But Not All Over You 114
Having a Coach 120
Don't Be Afraid to Claim Your Blessings 126
In Conclusion 131
A Word to the Ladies 138
About the Author 150

YOUR MINDSET IS YOUR SUPERPOWER OWN IT AND SOAR!

Show Up to RISE UP!

DR. MADELINE ANN LEWIS

FOREWORD

I have "Taken the Stage and OWNed it!" countless times with this incredible and quiet, subtle POWER HOUSE of a LEADER! I have had the honor, the pleasure and the treasure of working with Dr. Lewis for many years now. She has been a member of the Contributing Writer Team of "OWN It!" Magazine and Publishing as well as a Subject Matter Expert on the "OWN It!" Channel Live Shows; "It's Your Life OWN It!," "The Author's Corner", and "TCS Consulting Leadership and Organizational Development".

We started off as two women sharing a vision and mission, professional colleagues using our voices to change and transform the lives of our listeners/followers to becoming true sister-friends. It has been a humbling journey with Dr. Lewis, as we have worked together on leadership, organizational, and business development events, conferences both in person and virtual to ensure we achieved the results that were evident in impact and influence to all who participated and experienced it first-hand. Working together in collaborative publishing projects such as "OWN It!" Unapologetic a #1 Best-Seller in Professional Development. Dr. Madeline Ann Lewis, has poured out her expertise as a Trailblazer to open up the pathway for all who are willing to do the work to Show Up to RISE UP! There is no better more fulfilling way to live your life than to live a life poured out for the advancement of others. While her focus is on woman I know for sure there are men in her midst who have gleaned from all the nuggets she has shared over the years.

From "What Does Success Mean to You?" to "Harnessing the Power of Positive Thinking" to "Don't Be Afraid to Claim Your Blessings" Show Up to Rise Up is a book filled with everything you need to advance in your career. In today's dynamic

SHOW UP TO RISE UP!

professional landscape, the journey to success is both personal and multifaceted. "Show Up to Rise Up" addresses this complexity with a comprehensive exploration of critical themes, from defining your personal vision of success to grasping hold of the transformative power of positive thinking, and embracing the courage to claim your blessings.

"Show Up to Rise Up", serves as an invaluable resource, offering essential insights and practical strategies designed to empower individuals at every stage of their career. Whether you are seeking to refine your goals or cultivate a mindset conducive to growth, "Show Up to Rise Up" provides the tools necessary to advance and thrive in your professional endeavors. It is a guide for those ready to take proactive steps toward achieving their aspirations.

Cheers to another publication of a job well done! May you read every word with great expectations and Show Up! to RISE UP! to Take Center Stage and "OWN IT!" in your life, career, and business.

Marissa L. Bloedoorn

CEO TCS Consulting LLC.
Leadership/Organizational Development
CEO/Editor-in-Chief "OWN It!" Magazine & Publishing LLC.
Personal | Professional | Business Development
Multi-#1 Best Selling Anthologist in Self-Publishing

DR. MADELINE ANN LEWIS

ACKNOWLEDGEMENT

With Special Thanks:

To God be the Glory, thank You for the many blessings You have bestowed upon me and how far You have brought me. Thank You for allowing me to be a blessing and to make an impact on so many women. I am forever grateful and humbled to be able to share this book with all the ladies out there!

I could never put pen to paper without also thanking my Mom, for inspiring and encouraging me throughout my life. Your unwavering support has been my foundation, and I am deeply thankful for the strength you have instilled in me.

I also want to acknowledge and thank my Niece, who is mentioned in this book. I encourage you to always follow your dreams. I appreciate you not only as my Niece but as a person. I don't think you know just how kind-hearted you are. But trust me when I tell you the world and the people around you know. You are a beautiful person and young woman, and God has plans for you, believe He will use you in a mighty way.

To my family, who I can always call on for support and a strong shoulder, thank you for being there through every step of this journey.

I also want to extend my heartfelt thanks to Bishop Tom Watson and my cousin, Pastor Patricia Watson (Watson

Show Up to Rise Up!

Memorial Teaching Ministries). Your ministry and spiritual teachings keep me on track. Thank you for teaching the Word of God so clearly and concisely. I thank God for using you both in a mighty way. It is an honor to be under your spiritual guidance.

To my incredible staff, thank you for your unwavering support and for handling situations independently and without complaints. I could not have completed this book without your help and dedication.

A special thanks to Dr. Eric Kelly, III, a friend and colleague who gave me a platform that provided the opportunity to reach out to many. Thank you for your endless hours of mentoring and coaching, and for providing valuable business insight.

And to my close friends, thank you all for believing in me. Thank you for your prayers, encouragement, and patience. Thank you for giving me the time and space when I turned down your invitations to hang out, allowing me to get this project done. You have all sown seeds into my life that will produce a great harvest.

And finally many thanks, to every woman who reads these words…remember that within you lies the power to rise above any challenge, to create the life you desire, and to influence the world around you. This book is a testament to the strength and resilience we all possess. Let it serve as a reminder that no dream is too big, no goal is too far out of reach. Trust in your journey, keep your faith strong, and always show up to rise. Your mindset truly is your superpower.

Dr. Madeline Ann Lewis

DR. MADELINE ANN LEWIS

INTRODUCTION

WE ARE ALL ON A JOURNEY. We are all traveling regardless of age, occupation, gender, or race. This book looks at our journey, where we are heading, how we are getting there, and how we can improve our travel technique to ensure our journey is enjoyable and our arrival successful. Robert Louis Stevenson said that "... to travel hopefully is a better thing than to arrive, and the true success is to labor".

There are times in our journey when the going becomes difficult, when we may even lose our way. When this happens how can we persevere? What do we need to keep going?

What steps can we take to improve our quality of life? Do we need a magic wand or are the answers much simpler and closer to home?

We could link up with others for advice and support. Or we could take the brave but correct step and face up to our responsibilities and tackle our problems head on. We can do away with those things which slow us down and prevent us from reaching our true potential.

We can become our own person and a strong one at that. We can acquire the simple skills which help us step up to greater challenges and reap rewards we may never have even dreamed of.

One of the greatest weaknesses may be our lack of a

Show Up to RISE UP!

vision. Seeing your goals allows you to create a program whereby you can reach those goals. Having a program allows you to take specific steps. It might be you face a long journey but many a long journey is made up of simple, small steps.

Show Up to Rise Up is just that; a book to help you discover the inner you and to release your natural energy in such a way that your life will be changed markedly, for good and forever. This is a book which shows you how to lose those things which stifle your journey through life and take on board positive attitudes and beliefs which make both the journey and the arrival so much sweeter and beneficial.

All aboard…the journey starts now!

DR. MADELINE ANN LEWIS

A PERSONAL NOTE!

THIS IS YOUR TIME!

To every woman reading this book, I want you to know that "this is your time", the time is now to start your journey to success. The scripture says in Ecclesiastes 3:1, "To everything there is a season, a time for every purpose under heaven." This is your season to move, to create, to discover, to show up, and to rise up.

You are not here by accident. There is a purpose and a plan for your life that is unique to you. I pray that this book will enhance your life, giving you a deeper understanding of yourself and the immense value of the gifts you hold within. The world is waiting for what only you can bring.

Now is the time to create an abundant life, a life that reflects the brilliance, strength, and beauty that resides in you. You are prepared to do so, you have always been worthy to do so, and you deserve to do so. Go forward with confidence, knowing that you are equipped with everything you need to live the life God has planned for you.

May all of God's peace, purpose, and success be upon you as you embark on this incredible journey. Remember, you are powerful, you are capable, and you are destined to rise.

MUCH SUCCESS IN ALL YOUR ENDEAVORS,

Dr. Madeline Ann Lewis

Show Up to RISE UP!

DR. MADELINE ANN LEWIS

Defining Success

WHAT DOES SUCCESS MEAN TO YOU?

CHAPTER 1

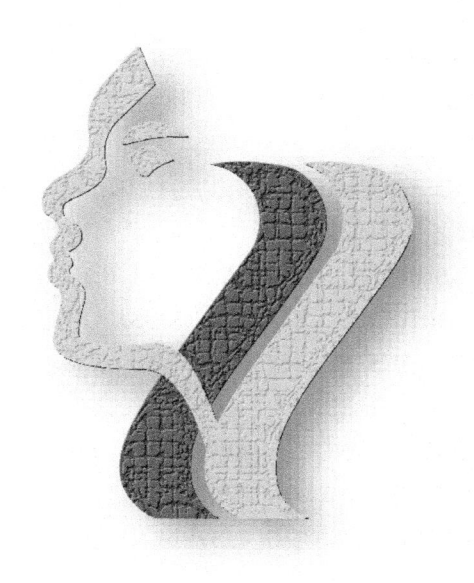

DEFINING SUCCESS
WHAT DOES SUCCESS MEAN TO YOU?

"Success is liking yourself, liking what you do, and liking how you do it."

Maya Angelou

WHAT IS YOUR DEFINITION OF SUCCESS? Contrary to what you might believe, it is different for every single person. Some people think success is a matter of financial stability or a certain amount of income.

In contrast, others may refer to success as personal happiness or even professional accomplishment. The truth is, there is no one-size-fits-all definition for success. There are even societal versus personal definitions of success.

Think back to when you were growing up. How did people around you define success? Often, we can base our perception of success on how others around us talked about it, worked for it, or even helped others achieve their own level of accomplishment. It is important to understand where these influences come from and what they did to our own definition of success.

If you need clarification on your definition of success, let's explore some diverse explanations for what this means to people. Whether you think success is more about your career, personal life, or even about your health, chances are, you'll align with one of these categories below.

THE MANY DEFINITIONS OF SUCCESS

Success doesn't have to be defined as a single goal of earning a million dollars or having the most lavish house in the neighborhood. It can be some people's version of success, but it is not the same for everyone.

For most people, this is far from what they think success is. Success is mainly defined by four specific areas of life achievement: career success, personal success, health and well-being, and financial success.

PROFESSIONAL SUCCESS: ACHIEVING CAREER MILESTONES

The most common type of success people often discuss pertains to your profession or your career. And it often is thought to be associated with lots of long hours at the office. As Vidal Sassoon says, "the only place where success comes before work

SHOW UP TO RISE UP!

is in the dictionary." That's certainly the case with the professional definition of success!

Career success is precisely what you might expect: achieving a certain level of leadership, finally starting that business that you desire feeling satisfied in the job that you are in, or even attaining professional recognition.

Women who aspire to achieve career success work to become the CEO of a major corporation, or they may even find themselves drawn to start businesses related to their passions. One of the best examples is Mary Barra, who was the CEO of General Motors.

Over the years, she was able to work her way up through engineering and administrative roles, eventually becoming CEO. During her tenure, she was applauded not only for her leadership and strategic decisions but also for prioritizing company culture and fostering a diverse, inclusive, and innovative workspace that redefined success.

Through her efforts, she created an environment where everyone thrives, leading to tremendous overall success for the entire organization at General Motors. The organization was completely changed because of her leadership.

DR. MADELINE ANN LEWIS

On the other end of the spectrum, regarding entrepreneurship, Sara Blakely is an excellent example. She was the founder of Spanx, who started her journey with only $5,000 in savings and a revolutionary idea for new women's undergarments. To most people, her idea seemed far-fetched, but she knew she had to try.

Despite the numerous rejections that she faced from her manufacturers and investors, her determination and innovation led her to create a billion-dollar business. Through her example, we see that success is about perseverance and creativity even when faced with challenges because, in the end, you can and will see success.

PERSONAL SUCCESS: FINDING SATISFACTION IN LIFE'S BALANCE

On the other hand, those who see success as a matter of personal success relate to the feeling of accomplishment in terms of their family relationships, friendships, personal growth, or even a work-life balance.

If you find yourself satisfied with achieving a certain social harmony with those around you while also working towards becoming a better version of yourself, you may align with this definition of success.

Show Up to Rise Up!

Arianna Huffington, the co-founder of *The Huffington Post*, is a great example of how you can attain success through achieving a work-life balance. Her success in the media is well known, but she also balanced her career with family life.

After a series of challenges, she ultimately chose to prioritize her well-being and family, which gave her greater life satisfaction. While she did not have professional success to the extent of others, she achieved another goal many of you might desire the most: a balanced, fulfilling life.

HEALTH SUCCESS: SUPPORTING OPTIMAL HEALTH

Health and well-being are other areas in which many define success, one that relates to your holistic health or physical, mental, emotional, or psychological health. This is defined by how well you care for yourself, and how much you support your longevity.

When you consider models, fitness experts, or others even in the neighborhoods around you constantly working towards the next fitness accomplishment, you can see examples of this diverse definition of success in practically any part of the world.

Taraji P. Henson, an actress and mental health

advocate, is well known for her own roles in TV and films, but she's also a great example of success in health and well-being. While speaking openly about her own struggles, she felt compelled to create the Boris Lawrence Henson Foundation, which supports mental health for the African American community.

Her level of success was not defined by any monetary amount or position in a company but rather by her own focus on health, which could resonate with many of you. Your health is, after all, the foundation of your life, so defining your success by your health is always a great idea.

FINANCIAL SUCCESS: ENJOYING STABILITY AND SECURITY

Finally, the most common definition of success is financial success, which can be defined or even with more complexity. For example, many people see financial success as achieving financial independence, accumulating a certain amount of money, or even enjoying financial security. On the other hand, people might say success is feeling as though every desire and need is taken care of with ease.

Bola Sokunbi is the Founder of Clever Girl Finance and a shining example of financial success. Clever Girl Finance was created to help women take control of their finances, inspired by Sokunbi's own background where money was taboo. Instead of letting this be her reality, she educated herself, budgeted, and invested, eventually achieving financial independence. From there, she educated others, too, giving them the tools to be successful.

Her example shows that you don't have to have millions or a large mansion to succeed. Sometimes, all it takes is skills and the tools to empower yourself to control your own financial situation. Your definition of success in terms of finance can be a matter of feeling empowered, rather than achieving a certain amount of money.

No matter which version of success you align with the most, it's important for you to understand what motivates you, what your goals are, and how you can achieve them. Once you recognize this, you'll be able to take steps to truly become the best version of yourself and accomplish the goals that you have set out for yourself, much like various women around the world today.

MORE INSPIRATIONAL STORIES OF SUCCESSFUL WOMEN

There are amazing examples of successful women worldwide who have achieved certain levels and types of success. Take, for example, Oprah

Winfrey. She grew up in poverty, facing significant challenges like abuse in her early life. Despite these challenges, she rose from being a local news anchor to one of the most recognizable global media moguls.

Her success is not just in media but across multiple industries. She also uses her position to empower and educate people, constantly advocating for issues that she feels passionate about.

She is the true definition of a rags-to-riches story, one that illustrates that overcoming adversity through resilience and staying true to one's passion and purpose will always lead to exceptional results.

With Michelle Obama, we see success stories that show the power of values-driven career transitions. Michelle Obama was once a successful corporate employee who switched to a more fulfilling career in social work.

She eventually left a high-paying corporate law job to become part of the public service industry while working to advocate for change. Her decision to make this monumental shift from one industry to the next demonstrates an alignment with personal values and broader goals, even if it didn't make sense to others around her.

Show Up to Rise Up!

Arguably, without her change to public service and advocacy, she would never have become the First Lady we all know today. This demonstrates that true success often means finding ways to become further aligned with who we are, what we care about, and how we want to impact the world.

If you are creative, there are still plenty of success stories from women across the globe. J.K. Rowling is one of the most famous examples of success.

She remained aligned and focused on completing the *Harry Potter* series, which has become one of the most popular fantasy series of all time. However, she didn't start out with mass amounts of success but with several trials and tribulations that she had to overcome.

In her trials and tribulations, she endured significant financial hardships as a single mother on welfare, often working in cafes and writing on napkins, working multiple jobs just to make ends meet.

Even despite the uncertainty, struggles, and doubts that she may have had, she still was able to achieve significant success. She shows us that even in the face of uncertainty, pursuing your passion is always the right decision to reach the level and type of success you aspire for.

Dr. Madeline Ann Lewis

Now that we've examined a few examples of success and the types of success you may align with, let's discuss defining your version of success, considering your values and personal goals, and looking beyond what society may tell you to do.

HOW TO DEFINE YOUR VERSION OF SUCCESS

Fortunately, you don't have to be a rocket scientist to define your version of success. In fact, you don't even have to use the definitions that we've described in this chapter alone.

What matters the most is that you define what success means to you. It would help to understand precisely what you want to achieve and how this leads to your life satisfaction.

To properly understand your version of success, there are a few key areas that you can look to. The first—and arguably the most important—is your core values.

What really matters to you? Is it your family, career, health, or personal hobbies? You have to define what values matter to you and how you can align with these in every action you take.

For example, if you value health and well-being, take steps daily to drink enough water, move your

Show Up to Rise Up!

body, and work towards your fitness goals. Your personal goals are another way to define your version of success, even beyond going to the gym.

When setting personal goals, you should always set SMART goals. Of course, you should set wise goals because they are tasks that will lead you to your aspirations. But the acronym SMART stands for five simple qualifiers that can help you create more achievable goals:

- Specific
- Measurable
- Attainable
- Relevant
- Time-bound

An example of a SMART goal is the following:

I will improve my public speaking skills by completing a six-week public speaking course and delivering at least three presentations to different audiences within the next eight weeks. This will involve dedicating three hours each week to attending the course, practicing, and preparing my talks.

As you can see, your goal contains specific information, is measurable, attainable, relevant to your path, and time bound. If you set goals like this, you'll have no problem achieving every milestone you set for yourself!

Dr. Madeline Ann Lewis

Finally, after you understand your core values and define your personal goals, it's essential to think beyond societal expectations. The truth is that success is not the key to your happiness, but happiness is the key to your success. If you love what you're doing, you will eventually be successful because of the passion and dedication you put into each and every hour you spend on the task.

Don't let yourself get bogged down by how society defines success. As long as you feel satisfied with your progress and where you're headed, with clear and reasonable goals, there's no reason you won't achieve the level of success that you desire.

Show Up to RISE UP!

DR. MADELINE ANN LEWIS

UNDERSTANDING
Positive Thinking

Harnessing the Power of Positive Thinking?

CHAPTER 2

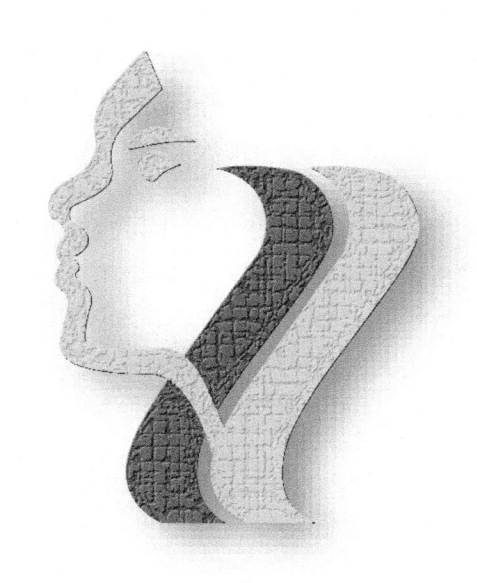

SHOW UP TO RISE UP!

UNDERSTANDING POSITIVE THINKING
HARNESSING THE POWER OF POSITIVE THINKING

"The only limit to our realization of tomorrow is our doubts of today." -**Franklin D. Roosevelt**

ARE YOU A GLASS-HALF-FULL OR HALF-EMPTY KIND OF PERSON? The answer to this question can tell you a lot about how you think about the world and how regularly you engage in positive thinking.

Positive thinking is the practice of focusing on the good in any situation. It's about something other than whether or not there is good in the problem, but what you think about what's happening.

You could be surrounded by adversity, challenges, and barriers that you must continually overcome, but being positive is a decision only you can make. If you are a glass-half-full person, being positive may come naturally to you.

However, if you are a glass-half-empty kind of person, then it's likely harder for you to think happy, positive thoughts regularly. In that case, it isn't easy to see the positive in a situation that could be interpreted as the opposite.

DR. MADELINE ANN LEWIS

THE TRANSFORMATIVE POWER OF POSITIVE THINKING

People often need to understand just how important optimism is, not only for how they view the world but also for their psychological health. You'd be surprised precisely how beneficial it can be to think positively.

People who think positively improve their mental health, reduce their stress, and even enjoy enhanced physical well-being. Some people even live longer as a result of thinking more positively about the situations they encounter on a daily basis!

You would be hard-pressed to find someone who thinks negatively standing on the Olympic stage competing at such a high level of competition. Similarly, people who are not positive often find it more challenging to achieve success in their own lives.

But it's not just about the physical or psychological benefits that you can achieve or even being as successful as someone like an Olympic athlete. Being more positive can help people in several other ways.

SHOW UP TO RISE UP!

Even in your own career, even for those who do not define success as career-oriented, you can achieve so much more if you remain focused on seeing the glass as half full. The more optimistic you are, the more you will notice opportunities when they arise, and the more it will benefit your performance.

While working professionally, being positive can help you become more resilient and creative. It can even help you improve the relationships you have with your coworkers and those in your life. In the long term, consider what this can do for your career and personal satisfaction!

THE SCIENCE BEHIND POSITIVE THINKING

Did you know that there are studies that demonstrate that positive thinking can actually benefit our brains? It's true! The brain's ability to form new connections is dependent upon how positive we are and how we think about the world around us.

In other words, our thoughts literally change the brain structure and function, allowing us to form new neural connections, even long after we have grown up from children to adults. It's incredible to think about the power of a single positive thought or even a collection of similar, optimistic thoughts.

These new neural connections are meaningful because they can help us encourage more neuroplasticity, which, over time, allows us to learn and grow. The more positive you are, the more likely you are to continually learn and develop to become the person you are meant to be. And the more you grow, the more you embrace your fullest potential.

The most optimistic individuals in the world tend to perform better in their careers simply because of this fact alone, and they also have more fulfilling personal lives. If you have ever walked into work in a positive mood, you can recall several moments when you saw the power of positive thinking.

Since there is such significant research to back this up, how on Earth can you encourage more positive thinking? Even if you find yourself surrounded by negative situations and challenges that push you and could make it harder to think more positively, there are several ways to focus on happier, more optimistic things throughout your day-to-day life.

TIPS AND TRICKS TO ENCOURAGE MORE POSITIVITY IN YOUR LIFE

It's not hard to encourage more positivity in your life, but it takes effort—and potentially a few happy accidents turned into heartwarming memories. The most important thing is not to be the thorn in your side that makes it hard to get through the day.

Maya Angelou had a saying that you might resonate with at times: "I've learned that even when I have pains, I don't have to be one." If you're having a bad day, it's a good reminder that it might just be our negative outlook bringing us down! All it takes is changing how we see what's happening, which is easy with these tips. I remember hearing Lia White, a brilliant young lady who said, "If you change the way you look at things, the things you look at will change."

TIP #1:
WRITE POSITIVE AFFIRMATIONS

When in doubt or in a rut, there are several tips and tricks for encouraging sunny, happier perspectives. The first, and arguably one of the most transformative, is writing down affirmations.

If you struggle with negative self-talk or thoughts, take time every day to write down positive thoughts about yourself and your goals. It might seem forced at first, but over time, it will come naturally to you. They could be the following:

I am intelligent, confident, and capable of achieving

my dreams.

I always know how to overcome the challenges that I face.

Even statements as simple as this can reinforce positivity in your world, giving you a new outlook even when the skies may seem gray. Reinforcing these happy thoughts will change the way you see yourself and all that's around you.

TIP #2:
PRACTICE GRATITUDE JOURNALING

You can also try gratitude journaling. This is an excellent opportunity to really focus on the things that you're grateful for. I recommend starting with writing down three things that you're grateful for every single day because it trains your brain to focus on the positives.

Over time, you'll notice that you'll begin to focus on the positives more than the negatives. It won't happen overnight, but it will happen if you are consistent. The compound effect of gratitude journaling can be gratifying, leading to you always seeing the glass as half-full, not half-empty. That's when you'll know that it's working!

TIP #3: VISUALIZE YOUR FUTURE

Visualization exercises are another great way to focus on the positives. You don't even have to spend too long on this, either. And you also don't need to be in a particularly positive situation to be able to visualize positives.

You can spend a few minutes every day visualizing your goals. Think about the positive outcomes you desire. Focus on how happy you feel. Even if you are not where you want to be yet, envision where you desire to end up, what goals you want to achieve.

All of this will make you feel even more encouraged and inspired, helping you eliminate those negative thoughts in the back of your head. The more you visualize, the more you can feel the satisfaction and feel motivated to continue towards your dreams.

TIP #4: USE MINDFULNESS MEDITATION

Some people also find meditation and mindfulness a great source of positivity. You can start your day with a short meditation session to center yourself and positively approach the day. Even just five minutes can give you a chance to reconnect with yourself.

You can also take mindful breaks throughout the day to breathe and focus on the present moment.

These little breaks will help you recenter yourself if you find yourself becoming more negative in the face of challenges. This can help you feel less stressed and give you a better outlook.

TIP #5:
GIVE YOUR SPACE A MAKEOVER

When in doubt and no other methods seem to be working, cultivating a positive environment is a great step in the right direction. After all, if your space is cluttered and you don't feel satisfied when you look around, you're likely not going to feel as positive about your situation.

That's why you should take time to declutter and decorate, creating a space that truly reflects how you want to feel. The more comfortable you feel in your own space, the more positive and supported you'll feel, too.

If you are creative, finding opportunities to create a space that inspires you is another way to tap into more positivity and encourage a beneficial outlook. Better yet, once you create these spaces, invite friends over who uplift and inspire you.

At the same time, focus on eliminating the negative influences from your life. Negative people and situations can really drain your energy, so it's best to avoid these at all costs!

TIP #6:
PERFORM DAILY ACTS OF KINDNESS FOR OTHERS

One final tip to help you encourage more positivity in your life is to perform random acts of kindness daily. This will not only help you feel better about impacting somebody else's life, but it can also change how you look at the world. It could be as simple as holding the door for a neighbor or buying coffee for a friend occasionally.

OVERCOMING NEGATIVE SITUATIONS

"An optimist is someone who gets treed by a lion but enjoys the scenery." -**Walter Winchell**

As much as we want to avoid it, there will be negative situations in our lives. It's impossible to have a solely positive existence without any hurdles or barriers to overcome. If we did have a positive existence without any challenges or negative situations to encounter, we would definitely not be the same people, nor would we appreciate all the good things in our lives.

Overcoming negative situations is important, and that's why positive thinking is such a powerful tool. You can probably think of multiple individuals who have encountered the worst conditions imaginable. Take Imprecina, a female entrepreneur who faced numerous business failures.

She continued trying different business models, but she failed every time, nearly five times in a row, having to start over and recuperate after each attempt. Even despite these challenges, she remained optimistic. She had affirmations on her wall and kept telling herself the following idea would be the one.

Eventually, she was right. She created a successful business that could be franchised in her local area. Even for those of us who are parents, it can be challenging to navigate the challenges of parenting and your career. Even when it seems complicated to find a balance, we can always take a step back and remember the positives.

Think back to the moments of gratitude, the connections you have with your family and friends, or even the achievements you have made in your professional life. All of this is proof enough that positive thinking and remaining optimistic are worth it because we all eventually overcome the challenges we're presented with.

CULTIVATE A POSITIVE MINDSET ONE DAY AT A TIME

Show Up to Rise Up!

Cultivating a positive mindset does not happen overnight. It takes effort and continuous focus to reframe negative thoughts. However, you can eventually have a more positive outlook as long as you maintain the right attitude, prioritizing positivity over negativity.

Mindset is essential because, without the right mindset, you'll continually see the glass as half empty when it is half full the entire time.

More importantly, it's all about daily habits. Whether you create a gratitude journal, write affirmations, or even perform daily acts of kindness, these small habits can shift your mindset significantly.

Cultivating a positive mindset is about seeing the world with a fresh perspective and always believing that the best is yet to come. As we explored, thinking more positively has many long-term benefits.

In your personal life, thinking more positively can create better relationships with others and allow you to connect with people on a deeper level. Even professionally, being more positive will enable you to encourage more success in your career, leading to new levels of achievement that you may desire.

Dr. Madeline Ann Lewis

As long as you commit daily to being more positive, you'll be able to harness the power of positive thinking and reap the benefits of seeing the glass as half full rather than half empty.

"Keep your face always toward the sunshine—and shadows will fall behind you." -**Walt Whitman**

Show Up to RISE UP!

GOAL SETTING AND ACHIEVING DREAMS
Why Are Goals Important
CHAPTER 3

DR. MADELINE ANN LEWIS

GOAL SETTING AND ACHIEVING DREAMS
WHY ARE GOALS IMPORTANT?

"Set your goals high, and don't stop till you get there." - **Bo Jackson**

WHAT WOULD YOU DO if you knew you could achieve anything? If you knew there was no limit to what you could accomplish, you would likely have a list of dreams and goals you wanted to achieve. It is in this imaginative headspace we can identify goals to work towards.

Goal setting is so important if you want to achieve your aspirations, not just because it gives you an end in mind but also because it can help you chart a pathway to completing little tasks along the way that lead you to this ultimate destination.

When we wanted to go to the moon, we didn't think about the limitations that forced us to stay on Earth. We started with the ultimate goal of getting to the moon, then identified all the steps that it would take for us to achieve getting into outer space, landing on the moon, and taking a moonwalk.

Just as the lion does not eat its entire meal in one

bite, you can't achieve a goal simply by doing it all at once. Setting goals is essential to help you understand where you're headed, but it can also help you stick to the promises that you have made for yourself. And when used appropriately, it can keep you on track and focused on taking it one day at a time.

HOW GOALS CAN HELP YOU

What is the essential ingredient that can propel a person to success? What is the special key that can unlock untold doors? What is the tool that can help mold your future? Well, it's simple yet greatly misused and misunderstood. It is a goal.

A goal is a dream with a time frame attached to it. Goals are stepping-stones to reach our dreams. If we can concentrate on our goals and learn how to set them and how to reach them, we can reach exceptional heights. That's where goal setting comes in, and why goals are so important.

Only some people are excellent at goal setting without much practice. While you're reading this, you're likely already thinking of people who do this without much effort. If you're skeptical about goal setting, think about the most successful people you know.

These individuals know exactly what they want to

achieve, even to the point where they can visualize it. Do you not think that they practiced goal setting so that they could achieve their accomplishments? Everyone who accomplishes something had to start with goal setting, or at least identifying what they wanted and how to get there.

Goals can help you in several ways, most notably by helping you become clear about what you can focus on. Take a marathon runner, for example. If a marathon runner goes into the race with no goal in mind, preparing without any expectation of what they need to achieve, it'll be tough for them to finish the race with confidence and within the time frame they need to.

You need to focus on clarity regarding your goals, just as the marathon runner knows precisely how long and how far they need to run. When you have clear goals, you know exactly what direction you're headed in, making it exceedingly easy for you to go forth confidently.

Not only are goals incredibly helpful for providing clarity, focus, and direction, but they're also important for your personal and professional growth. Goal setting can drive growth and allow you to achieve significant milestones.

You may want to become a yoga instructor, but it can be hard to grow and achieve these milestones

Show Up to Rise Up!

if you are still determining what you need to accomplish to get there. On the other hand, setting a goal of achieving a certain program and completing the steps to receive the certification within a certain time frame will allow you to grow professionally and personally.

Each and every step you take to achieve a goal allows you to become more resilient, confident, and self-assured with the path that you're on. Just like when you were younger—whether it was working towards goals for school, sports, or even college—goal setting can make you a better, stronger, more prepared individual.

Goals can also help you avoid looking like you're running around like you're stuck in a maze. When you're in a maze, you have no idea where you're going, no direction, and no way of orienting yourself. This can leave you feeling extremely apprehensive and frustrated.

That's why it is so important to set goals: to have a clear vision and expectation of where you're headed. Now, let's look at how you can set up these goals using the previously discussed acronym.

SETTING EFFECTIVE GOALS:
Step-by-Step Guide to SMART Goals

DR. MADELINE ANN LEWIS

Setting practical goals is about knowing exactly what kind of goals to set. You can focus on any area of your life when it comes to goal setting, but the best way to set a goal is to make it a SMART goal. SMART stands for **S**pecific, **M**easurable, **A**ttainable, **R**elevant, and **T**ime-bound. They are intelligent goals and straightforward about what you need to achieve.

SPECIFIC

When setting goals, the first thing to focus on is being specific. You can only say that you want to become a better basketball player if you are particular about what you need to focus on. Your goal should be clear and exact, giving you an evident and easily understood idea in your mind.

For example, you might want to become a better basketball player but to be more specific; you want to focus on improving your free throws.

MEASURABLE

The next step is to ensure that your goals are measurable. Measurable goals allow you to measure your progress over time. For example, if you want to improve your engagement on social media or have an Instagram page, you wouldn't say that you just want to focus on improving your engagement.

SHOW UP TO RISE UP!

To create a measurable goal, you want to increase your engagement by 10%. This will give you a way to quantify your progress so that you can see exactly how far you've come and where you need to go to achieve your aspirations.

ACHIEVABLE

The next step in creating a SMART goal is to ensure it's realistic and attainable. If you are starting to learn a language, it might not be achievable to say that you can be fluent in Mandarin within six months.

It would help if you were realistic but still make it an achievable goal. Suppose you said instead that you wanted to achieve fluency in Mandarin within three years. In that case, this is a much more attainable goal that will not intimidate you from even trying to accomplish it.

RELEVANT

Relevance is another critical part of creating SMART goals. You can't make a goal for running a marathon if you're training to become a swimmer. Your goal should align with your aspirations. More specifically, if we're talking about career and life objectives, then your goals should make sense for where you are.

For example, if you are in the marketing industry, you may aim to become a manager in your department in the next year. It wouldn't make sense if you're in marketing to want to aspire to become an accountant if you do not have the skills to do so.

TIME-BOUND

Finally, the last step in creating goals you can achieve, and measure is ensuring they are time-bound. Your goals should have a deadline in mind, not so you have to reach them but so that you know exactly how long you want them to take.

Some of the best time-bound goals include completing certification courses by the end of the year for your specific profession or even being able to run a marathon within a certain number of months.

Don't let the deadline freak you out! The deadline is simply a measurable objective that you have. If you miss out and you're unable to achieve the goal, it doesn't mean you fail if it takes you longer. It just means you finally need some extra time to reach that point.

With these tips, you can easily create effective goals that will help you achieve your aspirations over time. However, here's some advice to help you stay on track and motivate yourself even if you have yet to get closer to achieving each goal you've set for yourself.

PRACTICAL ADVICE FOR GOAL SETTING AND ACHIEVING YOUR GOALS

"Setting a goal to go to the gym is easy; it's the actual 'going' part that gets tricky."

No quote reasonably describes goal setting and achievement like the one above. Setting goals is the easy part, but actually achieving the goal is always the hardest part!

You probably know exactly what it feels like: if you're preparing to write a book, you likely already have a goal and when you want to complete the book. But setting aside the time to complete it, piece by piece, chapter by chapter, is the hardest part.

Here's how you can properly goal set to achieve your aspirations.

BREAK DOWN YOUR GOALS INTO DIGESTIBLE TASKS

If you want to set goals and achieve them, you should first break down the goals to maximize your efforts. For example, if you want to receive a promotion, you should start with smaller goals that can lead to this ultimate goal. For example, you might make it a mission to sign up for more projects at work to demonstrate your commitment, leading to promotion.

If you are trying to run a marathon, you might first start by being able to run a mile in a certain amount of time. You should be able to outline the steps piece by piece, giving yourself little tangible steps that you can take that'll give you a sense of accomplishment and help you get closer and closer to the ultimate end.

STAY FLEXIBLE AND ADAPTABLE

One of the worst things you can do for yourself is to remain stubborn when trying to achieve your goal. Ultimately, the plan you have in place initially will be different from what you need to fulfill your aspirations.

Be willing to adjust your goals as necessary because your circumstances and plans will change. If you are injured, for example, and trying to achieve a fitness goal like running a marathon, adjusting your fitness goals to become more appropriate for where you currently are is essential.

Stay focused, flexible, and adaptable, and you'll be

able to achieve almost anything.

CONSISTENCY IS KEY

Above all else, consistency is the most important tip for helping you set goals and achieve every aspiration. Making daily habits and committing to them are all part of the incremental progress you need to achieve that result.

Women like Oprah Winfrey and J.K. Rowling did not achieve what they did overnight, but they took daily steps to get there. For Oprah Winfrey, she continued to work harder and harder, finding opportunities to progress through the workplace. On the other hand, J.K. Rowling continued to write daily, finding a way to get her manuscript finished, edited, and published.

If you find ways to remain consistent, you will create daily habits that further promote your success and become a natural part of your day-to-day life.

THE CLARITY OF YOUR GOALS DETERMINES YOUR SUCCESS

The only limit we truly have is the one we place upon ourselves because of doubt, but as long as you set clear goals, you can determine your own level of success. The clearer you are about your goals and how you can achieve your ultimate aspirations, the more prepared you are for the path ahead.

No matter what happens, always remember: if you have the right mindset and goals, you can achieve anything you set your mind to!

Show Up to Rise Up!

Overcoming Obstacles and Building Resilience
The Key to Professional and Personal Growth

CHAPTER 4

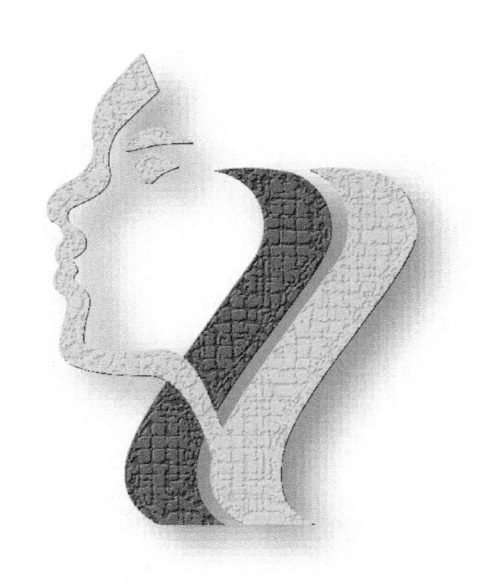

Dr. Madeline Ann Lewis

OVERCOMING OBSTACLES AND BUILING RESILIENCE: THE KEY TO PROFESSIONAL AND PERSONAL GROWTH

"I can be changed by what happens to me. But I refuse to be reduced by it." **Maya Angelou**

OBSTACLES ARE CHALLENGES WE ALL FACE, but how we manage them shares a lot about our character and how resilient we are. You likely avoid obstacles and challenges as much as possible. It's only natural. However, if you avoid the obstacles that allow you to become the person you're meant to be, success is even harder.

Overcoming obstacles and building resilience because of it is the key to professional and personal growth, no matter how you want to slice it. It's the classic case of tripping on a flat surface.

We have all stumbled, whether we handle it gracefully or not, but how we get up after falling determines the level of resilience we cultivate, which directly impacts our ability to accomplish what we have set out to do.

Several obstacles might arise in your life. Many of

us, especially women, relate to similar challenges in the workplace.

IDENTIFYING COMMON OBSTACLES IN THE WORKPLACE

In the workplace, there are several common barriers or issues that you might face. The obstacles can look quite similar for women, even despite different industries or workplaces.

For instance, gender bias is a major challenge, one that can lead to significant discrimination and challenges in terms of how quickly you experience promotions and recognition at work. If you have ever felt like you have been overlooked because of your gender, then you may have been exposed to gender bias in the office.

Another area many people need help with is the struggle to maintain a work-life balance. Our careers can take up so much of our lives. However, what about the precious moments you desire to have with your family?

Achieving a balance between professional and personal contexts is essential, especially if you want to build resilience and continue to grow as a person.

Finally, you have likely heard of the most

common and discussed challenge: the glass ceiling. Much like gender bias, women often face challenges in reaching the glass ceiling.

This visible barrier separates them from others who achieve more workplace recognition promotions. While this has improved in recent years, there is still much to be done to make this even less of an issue for today's women professionals.

For example, Patricia's journey in engineering in the automotive industry was met with significant challenges, just like the obstacles we discussed. The automotive industry is predominantly made up of male professionals, but Patricia found herself interested in the sector.

Over the years, she was frequently ignored or dismissed but sometimes echoed by a male colleague. Despite these challenges, she continued developing her skills, volunteered for challenging projects, and sought mentorship from other supportive senior engineers who could guide her to achieve her career aspirations.

Fortunately, it all paid off when she led a groundbreaking project that revolutionized the company's approach to its products. Her success made her a top executive at the company, inspiring greater gender diversity and recognition that everyone can contribute meaningfully, even in a supposedly male-dominated industry.

Now that we've looked at professional obstacles let's explore the personal challenges you might face. In these moments, it's crucial you overcome these obstacles and build resilience to become an improved version of yourself.

OBSTACLES YOU FACE IN YOUR PERSONAL LIFE

We can all relate to personal challenges, such as feelings of inadequacy, financial challenges, or even health concerns. These issues affect every area of our lives, even beyond the four walls of our homes.

Self-doubt is a major obstacle that can lead us to either give up or feel forced to reconsider our path. Feelings of inadequacy or imposter syndrome, such as wondering if we're good enough to accomplish or take on the role that we have been assigned, are common occurrences that affect people of all ages.

On the other hand, financial struggles are shared among everyone, making us feel like we constantly have to work harder for stability and independence. Feeling as though we do not have enough money or desire more stability is a prevalent emotion we all face, but how we deal with this ultimately determines how resilient and strong we become as individuals.

Of course, we must discuss health issues. Health concerns like physical and mental health hurdles are necessary points where you must stop and consider if what you're doing is genuinely helping yourself or hurting your health.

Only with reflection and understanding of where we are and how we can support optimal health can we overcome these obstacles and achieve a healthier lifestyle.

In one hypothetical scenario, Kimberlee presents an exceptional model of how to overcome personal struggles and obstacles. Desiring to complete a marathon, she was riddled with self-doubt, especially believing that she could not physically complete the run.

Although she had always been less athletic, one day, she decided that she would go for it, even if she had doubts. She signed up for the race, training and finding herself pushed to the limit.

It was difficult for her to run more than a mile without getting to the point of exhaustion. Her negative thoughts constantly told her she wasn't good enough. However, instead of quitting, she sought help from a trainer.

Kimberlee joined a running club, continuing to complete each goal she set out for herself, passing each milestone easily. As she slowly built up her resistance, despite her anxiety, she was able to achieve 26.2 miles for her marathon.

This triumph over her self-doubt redefined how she looked at her life, showing her that with positive thinking and determination, she could accomplish anything she set her mind to.

To become like Kimberlee and Patricia, there are some strategies you can use to overcome challenges in your life, whether they be personal or professional.

STRATEGIES TO OVERCOME CHALLENGES

"The oak fought the wind and was broken, the willow bent when it must and survived." - **Robert Jordan**

Overcoming challenges and obstacles is about developing the right mindset, using practical tools, and leveraging your support systems. Let's explore each individually.

Developing the right mindset is important because, without the right outlook, you'll constantly be surrounded by negative thoughts and unable to progress. If you look through lenses that only highlight the negative parts of what's around you, then you're not going to see these challenges as opportunities for growth. You'll become the person who mistakes a molehill for a mountain, making the problem much worse than it actually is! Don't forget early on, I mentioned "if you change the way you look at things, the things you look at will change."

With the right and growth mindsets, you can see that every opportunity is a chance to learn. Embracing a growth mindset is about seeing that lemons can turn into lemonade and sometimes even a lemon pie!

Things will not always go as planned, but if you constantly view everything as an opportunity to grow and even laugh a little at the mistakes you make, you'll find your way to success.

Aside from adopting a growth mindset, a practical tool that you can use, at the risk of repeating myself, which we explored above, is SMART goals. These types of goals can help you navigate and overcome obstacles because they're specific and measurable, and they're also time-bound, so you know when you'll be able to achieve something.

Devising these goals involves some brainstorming and planning, but let's walk through an example. If

Show Up to Rise Up!

you want to run a mile in less than 8 minutes, you have to break down the situation step by step. You can't eat a meal all in one bite, so you shouldn't expect to reach under eight minutes instantly, either.

First, you would aim to run a mile in less than 10 minutes by a certain time frame appropriate for your fitness level. After that, you would continually work your way down until you reach 8 minutes or less.

If you make the goals approachable, relevant, measurable, specific, and oriented to a time frame that makes sense for you, you can problem-solve and strategically plan your way to success.

Finally, you should leverage your support systems to overcome challenging situations in your life. Networking within your professional circle is a great way to make friends, meet mentors, and keep in touch with colleagues. It is also a great opportunity to find people who can provide you with guidance and encouragement, even in the face of significant challenges.

You never know what connection will lead to your next career opportunity. For example, Celeste works in the information technology industry. Still, her connection to somebody in healthcare allowed her to find a job at a hospital with a higher-paying salary that aligned with her career goals and where she saw herself in the future.

With these three strategies, you can overcome challenges and continue to build resilience. However, let's look at three ways you can focus on building resilience daily.

TIPS TO BUILD RESILIENCE

If you want to build resilience, it's all about continuous learning, remaining adaptable, and practicing self-care. Life should be seen as a constant learning journey regardless, but with a concentrated focus on education, you can develop skills to help you overcome obstacles.

Continuous learning is essential to help us develop as individuals and work on our technical skills. If you are in management, learning more about marketing might be exactly what you need to secure the desired promotion. On the other hand, if you are in design, you might learn a new design technique to overcome a common obstacle you face in your day-to-day work.

Another tip to help you overcome your challenges to build resilience is to remain adaptable. Staying flexible is not just about being able to roll with the punches but also moving past negative situations. If you spill coffee in the morning on your way to

Show Up to Rise Up!

work and think your day is ruined, you're making yourself your own worst enemy.

During these moments, comic relief is necessary, and being flexible and adaptable is the key to overcoming the minor obstacle that you may have blown out of proportion. Even in the face of significant challenges, being flexible and adaptable can help you.

For example, if your entire team is restructuring, you have to be versatile and willing to think outside the box to ensure your department's success. Otherwise, it may lead

to more challenges than you expect. The more adaptable and flexible you become, the more resilient you are to change.

Finally, above all else, self-care is a huge part of staying and becoming more resilient over time. Managing stress, implementing certain self-care routines, and maintaining a work-life balance is critical to your health, mental health, and overall outlook.

Many of us may feel that we can juggle all that life throws at us. Yet, for others, we may look like circus performers who forget how to juggle, trying to balance work, hobbies, and even a social life. It's okay to admit that you can't do it all.

Sometimes, it's about doing what you can first.

It's essential always to consider your feelings and what you need because when you care for yourself, you can take care of everything else. Self-care is the foundation for success, but it's also the quiet moments that build resilience and help you nurture that determination and positive outlook you need for success.

FACE YOUR CHALLENGES AND BUILD RESILIENCE

We might not all be as revered as leaders and overcomers like Marie Curie, Serena Williams, or Malala Yousafzai, but we also have the challenges that we must face. When you understand that obstacles are necessary, whether personal or professional, you can identify them, face them in your personal life, and your strategies to overcome them and build resilience.

The more you challenge yourself and believe that each obstacle is just a learning opportunity, the better you will become as an individual and the more you can achieve in the future.

Show Up to Rise Up!

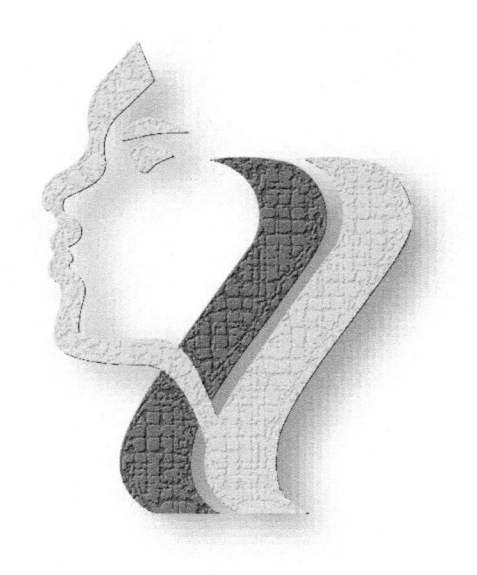

Achieving Balance and Cultivating Support
The Secret Ingredients
For Success
Chapter 5

Dr. Madeline Ann Lewis

ACHIEVING BALANCE AND CULTIVATING SUPPORT: THE SECRET INGREDIENTS FOR SUCCESS

"Balance is not something you find; it's something you create." **Jana Kingsford**

IF YOU WANT TO ACHIEVE BALANCE, you must understand the importance of discipline and leveraging those you know in your life who can help you. Just as Rome wasn't built in a day—or by a single person—you won't accomplish your goals without a little help from your friends and some discipline.

We will explore achieving balance and cultivating support, the secret ingredients for success. You don't need an entire army behind you as Rome had, but you need a select few individuals to help guide you, give you mentorship, and show you the way.

First, let's explore the role of self-discipline and continuous learning, two areas where you can contribute daily to help support your growth and development, to ultimately give you the skills and confidence you need to accomplish your dreams.

SHOW UP TO RISE UP!

THE ROLE OF SELF-DISCIPLINE AND CONTINUOUS LEARNING

Discipline remains the differentiator between those who succeed and those who do not. Jerry Seinfeld's "Don't Break the Chain" method is the best way to describe discipline. With an enormous daily calendar in front of him, each X he marked was for a day he wrote a job. The goal?

To catch every single day, create lines and lines of red X's. And he did, for a long time, in fact, and he credits most of his success to this daily effort. It's a method that people use worldwide today in varying capacities. If you do the same thing, keeping yourself committed to daily action towards your goals, you, too, can achieve the aspirations you have for yourself.

To practice self-discipline, set daily or weekly learning goals. You should think of it like feeding a goldfish because consistency matters most. Even if you do 5 minutes one day but 30 minutes the next, it's about consistency and setting aside the time to get this done.

Make sure you're clear about what you want to learn and be dedicated to the time you spend on it because even a concentrated, short burst of energy can lead to excellent learning potential.

DR. MADELINE ANN LEWIS

You can use apps, journals, and even physical calendars to track your progress. Do whatever aligns with you and what motivates you. The most important thing is to find a method that works for you that makes you excited to get up in the morning and get that task done.

And, of course, remember to celebrate the little victories. After you've reached a significant milestone, have a mini dance party or go out for a special dinner!

It's okay to celebrate before you achieve the big goal to celebrate. Every little milestone you reach is another proof of how far you've come and what your self-discipline is doing for your growth and development.

The first step is to identify one goal you want to work towards. Then, much like Jerry Seinfeld, grab that calendar or application and begin to mark off each day that you remain committed to this goal.

Before you know it, if you focus on daily effort, you'll reach dozens and dozens, if not hundreds of days, of consistent effort until you reach your desired destination.

Next, let's look at how cultivating support can be a great indicator of your success. It can even give you the tools and tricks that you need to learn from some of the best so you can skyrocket your progress and achieve your goals, both personally and professionally.

BUILDING A SUPPORT SYSTEM FOR SUCCESS

"Surround yourself with only people who are going to lift you higher." - **Oprah Winfrey**

As the saying goes, you are the average of the top five people you hang out with regularly. So, who do you reflect? Do you reflect people that are successful or want to be successful? Or do you reflect people who are negative, often pessimistic?

The importance of networking, mentorship, and building a strong and supportive community must be recognized and often under-discussed. The more connections you have, the more opportunities you have for your career and to learn new skills and explore new projects.

We can turn to individuals like Sheryl Sandberg, who has achieved professional success, to demonstrate the power of someone's network. Not only does she have the determination and skill set required for the jobs that she has performed, but she also leveraged her network, using mentors like Larry Summers and networking events to help her grow into the leader she has become.

She's not the only one to have achieved such significant success, a byproduct of her support system. You can turn to virtually any successful entrepreneur, executive, or even someone in your circle to see just how much mentorship, support circles, and networking can benefit you.

Reaching out to others may seem daunting, especially as you begin networking and connecting more than you have before. But it's important to remember to find people who match your aspirations. The best mentors and network connections are those with a similar path as you, ones who can inspire you to the next step of your journey, too.

You can work just like Sheryl Sandberg did, finding your own super mentor to guide you. Everyone deserves to have a great mentor to help them through their challenges, but sometimes, it takes a trip to find your mentor in your support circle or other networking groups.

You should actively seek mentors, whether through professional organizations, industry events, or even in your social circle, for personal growth. You can even have coffee dates and build a supportive circle with those you feel could contribute to your growth and development.

The first step is to identify people you believe would be worth talking to about mentorship and then reach out to them. See what they say, if not, keep searching for the perfect fit for someone to guide you through your industry or life challenges.

HOW TO MAINTAIN A BALANCED LIFESTYLE WITH SELF-CARE

"Take care of your body. It's the only place you have to live." - **Jim Rohn**

Maintaining a balanced lifestyle is not just about self-discipline and support but also about taking care of yourself. Your body is the only one you get, and how you take care of it directly indicates how healthy it will be in the future.

Arianna Huffington, whom we discussed in previous chapters, collapsed from exhaustion, leading to a personal overhaul of her entire life. It was her wake-up call to let her know that she didn't have to go all in, hurting her health and eliminating self-care, a necessary part of taking care of herself and still being able to achieve success.

Only after she decided to prioritize meditation, stress-relieving activities, and taking time away from work did she indeed see a more balanced and holistically healthy lifestyle. Similarly, you should also take steps to balance work and life because if you don't, you could unfortunately end up in a similar position to her.

To balance your lifestyle and encourage more self-care, schedule some downtime. Make sure that there's one day a week when you are not doing anything on your calendar. If you plan it as "me time," you might even feel more inclined to take time and enjoy it.

However, it's not just about taking these days to really reflect and allow yourself to relax; it's also about taking daily steps to encourage your health and well-being. Self-care is about moving your body every single day in a way that makes you feel good. It's about remaining mindful and practicing quiet moments to reflect and relax.

Not only that, but it's also about healthier steps, like eating a nutritious diet based on whole foods and setting clear boundaries with those in your life, potentially draining your energy. This doesn't have to be just people as well. This can also be commitments like work or personal decisions that you've made, ones that may not be the right decision for you.

As you consider how to take care of yourself and

SHOW UP TO RISE UP!

find more time for a balance lifestyle, start small with daily habits. Take steps to eat healthier, then set aside time to move your body more. After that, you can begin to plan self-care days every single week. As long as you take care of yourself daily, weekly, and monthly, you will see an improvement.

The goal should always be to find balance, never allowing yourself to work too hard on work while neglecting yourself, and vice versa. As always, take time to review and adjust your plan. How your body and *YOU* need to be taken care of at one point in your life will undoubtedly change in the future.

Even if you need to adjust your plans, any form of self-care is the right decision on the path to achieving balance and cultivating support. It gives you an opportunity and a better foundation to achieve all your goals and dreams.

WHEN YOU ACHIEVE BALANCE, YOU SUPPORT YOUR DREAMS

"Success is not the key to happiness. Happiness is the key to success. If you love what you are doing, you will be successful." **Albert Schweitzer**

Achieving balance is the key to achieving your dreams. If you find ways to remain self-disciplined, build a strong support system, and support yourself in your care, you will see a change in the trajectory of your life. However, most importantly, it's about finding happiness.

Your version of balance will not be the same as everybody else's, and that's something to keep in mind. Some people thrive on more focus on work, while others may need more time to reflect, rest, and enjoy life's quiet moments. All that matters is that you find what bounds work for you.

With an understanding of the self-discipline, you need to learn and develop continuously, you can prioritize the skills and opportunities you need to grow as an individual. Even if you are focused on your career aspirations less than yours, this will still help you in monumental ways.

Even in the most challenging times, your support network, and the mentorship you find with others ensure that your personal career development remains strong, even if you're self-development and self-discipline waver. Think of these individuals like a super mentor, constantly guiding you to the next step with wisdom so that you don't have to make the same mistakes they will do in the future.

Show Up to Rise Up!

Finally, even after you have mastered self-discipline and have a strong support network, you must always take time to take care of yourself. If you are not taking care of yourself, then you certainly are not able to take care of all that you have in store for yourself! Even if it's a few minutes to meditate or listen to your favorite song, don't forget to make sure you're happy, too.

After all, the journey to success is not always just about feeling accomplished when you get there. For most of us, it's the thrill of the journey and the beauty of all that we accomplish along the way, in those small moments when milestones are met, and our confidence increases with every step.

Dr. Madeline Ann Lewis

Direction and Destination

In Which Direction Are You Headed and Where Will You End Up?

CHAPTER 6

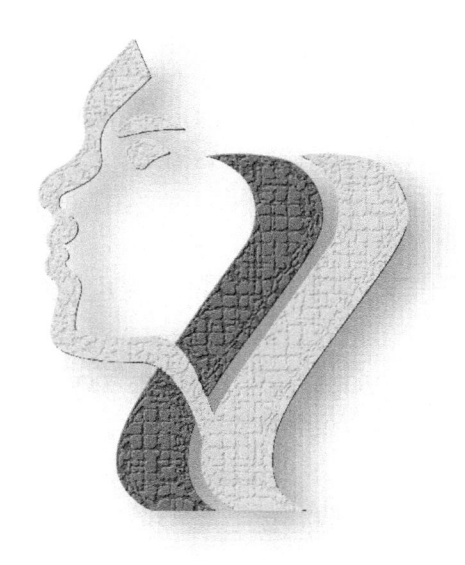

SHOW UP TO RISE UP!

DIRECTION AND DESTINATION: IN WHICH DIRECTION ARE YOU HEADED AND WHERE WILL YOU END UP?

T'S A SIMPLE FACT. You will end up where you are heading. If you get your direction-finder to work well, you give yourself an excellent chance of reaching your destination. But it becomes a chicken and egg situation. Which comes first, the chicken or the egg, the direction, or the destination?

If you know the direction you are traveling you can control your destination. If you know your destination, you can adjust your direction of travel.

DESTINATION DETERMINES DIRECTION

Let's begin with your destination. You need to list this, to make it a reality by writing the facts and having the words available for frequent consultation. Your destination could be

- a sense of well-being, your physical, emotional, and mental health or

- the acquisition of some thing or things such as a qualification, a skill, a property, a career or
- a mission such as being able to help others.

Whatever your destination, and it could be more than one thing, if you commit it to paper, you are giving yourself the prompt to continually think about it and thus plan accordingly. It is your destination which determines your actions. Once you know, *really* know, your destination, you are able to plan your mode of travel.

PREPARATION IS THE KEY

If you are going on a trip, you know you must prepare. You need money or access to money, the right type and amount of clothes, any special equipment such as skis or scuba gear, maps, contact names and addresses, tickets, passport, and a person back home who will feed your cat and check your mail while you are away. Failure to prepare or to prepare properly may make your trip a sad and difficult time.

So, your proposed trip is your proposed destination. Name it. Commit to paper the details of your destination. Place the written details where you can read them every day. Give it detail by adding flesh to the bones.

SHOW UP TO RISE UP!

A destination which states *I want to be happy* is self-defeating. Why do you want happiness? How will you know you have found it? What form will this happiness take? Be precise and detailed. Here is a fleshed-out example of a destination.

> I wish to learn to speak and write Italian.
> I wish to achieve fluency within 18 months.
> I wish to travel to Italy to meet my mother's family.
> I plan to travel in the summer of 2024.
> I will enroll in classes no later than February 1, 2024

DIRECTION REQUIRED

Once you have your specific destination, the direction will follow. In the example above, assuming you have little or no knowledge of speaking and writing Italian, you will need to take certain steps. So, there is a timeframe, a deadline for taking such steps. This timeframe is vitally important.

You can even add a monitoring program. List dates and what is to be achieved by each date e.g.

> March 1, 2024, Join local Italian society
> July 1, 2024, Pass Level 1 of *Learn Italian*
> October 1, 2024, Pass Level 2 of *Learn Italian*

DR. MADELINE ANN LEWIS

The monitoring program keeps you on track. It is easy to drift off target and fall behind in your journey. Regular checks are essential. Keeping a diary of your progress is also helpful. Weekly entries of what you've achieved give you a boost when you look back and see how far you've come. Then by adding mini goals for each week you further reinforce your direction. This is how I mapped out my plan to finish my dissertation for my doctorate degree.

FLEXIBILITY IS FINE

Many a journey can take much time. If you're starting from scratch, you won't be fluent in learning Italian in a week. So, as you travel and constantly review your progress, don't be afraid to make a change. Having the destination locked away is vital but it is possible to change your mode of travel en route.

You might think of a new tactic or action. You might find you are lagging behind or, better still, going past your markers and progressing really well. In this case a change in direction could be in order. Be willing and brave to make a change. Be flexible.

AVOID DISTRACTIONS

SHOW UP TO RISE UP!

We all have everyday activities in our lives be it a job, family, hobbies, pets or running for local government. The key is to *not* let these every day activities interrupt your travel. It may mean juggling activities and shifting tasks when we tackle something. But the key here is to keep going. If you miss a step in your journey because you or your Mom are suddenly taken ill, work hard later to get back on track. And where possible, avoid distractions.

If a friend has a habit of calling in and talking about nothing for ages, find a way around this distraction. Be out, be honest or be strong.

PULL DON'T PUSH

It's possible to travel one of two ways. You can be pushed from behind or you can be lead from in front. Go with the latter. Set your destination up in lights. Focus on it, daily if you can, and be drawn to that destination. Allow your dream to lead you on.

"Certainly travel is more than the seeing of sights; it is a change that goes on, deep and permanent, in the ideas of living."

-Miriam Beard

Anything Is Possible!

Perseverance, Determination, and Belief in Yourself

CHAPTER 7

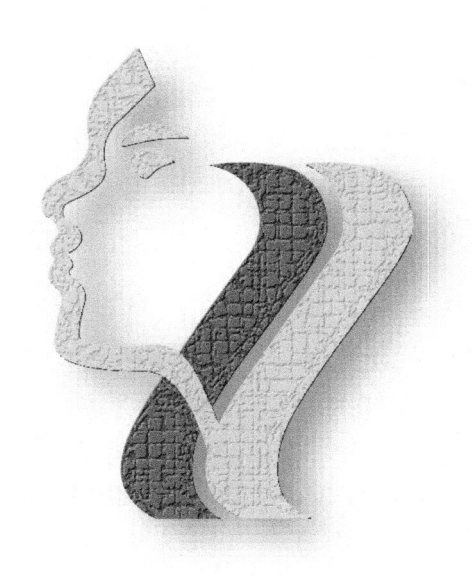

SHOW UP TO RISE UP!

ANYTHING IS POSSIBLE! PERSERVERANCE, DETERMINATION, AND BELIEF IN YOURSELF

"Life is not easy for any of us. But what of that? We must have perseverance and above all confidence in ourselves. We must believe that we are gifted for something, and that this thing must be attained."

-Marie Curie

IN MAKING YOUR PLANS, MAKE THEM BIG. One of the biggest obstacles to success is underestimating our own ability. We dream of a goal, and we wish for something but many of us do one of two things.

- We believe the goal or destination is unattainable and so never make any preparation in the first place or
- We make the preparation and start on the journey towards our destination but drop out mid-journey; we give up.

Both of these scenarios equal only one result – failure. But let's be positive. Let's take the alternative to failure, success.

So having dreamed our dream and stated our destination, we prepared for our journey. This brings us to three of the essential ingredients, three partners or pals, three tools which can guarantee our success. We're talking here about perseverance, determination, and self-belief.

PERSEVERANCE

Life is crammed with stories of people who have persevered. This means keeping on keeping on. How many inventors, writers, sportsmen and women, dancers, designers, and plain old ordinary folk have achieved something simply by perseverance? Millions.

There are famous folk such as Benjamin Banneker and Alexander Graham Bell who made breakthrough discoveries in science. Did they make their breakthroughs in the first week, month or year of their study and experimental work? No, it took many years of trial and error of striving to find the answers.

Both these scientists have left a lasting legacy of discovery for others to build on and for millions to benefit from. But in both cases, they stuck at their work, they persevered.

Then there are untold millions of ordinary folks who have set themselves a destination or goal and worked their sox off to reach that destination. It could be passing an exam, quitting smoking, or losing weight. But whatever the task these unknown people have achieved success. Did they have a magic ingredient?

Winston Churchill addressed the students at his former school and told the boys they should remember the three ingredients to success. They are

- Never give up
- Never give up
- Never give up

Churchill said you could fail with one of these ingredients and in fact could fail with two. But so long as you keep using just one of these three ingredients, you are bound to succeed. Persevere!

DETERMINATION

It might be difficult to define determination. Let's try from the point of view of a dictionary. Determination is a noun meaning *the act of coming to a decision or of fixing or settling a purpose.*

Notice the word *act* in the definition. To act on the stage or to act on an idea implies action, movement, the business of doing something. One of the biggest obstacles to success is inertia. Many of us are lazy. And it need not be bone-idle lazy. It might be that we procrastinate.

You know, the "I'll do that tomorrow or this afternoon or next week". We find excuses *not* to act. The very nature of being determined is to take action. Of course, you can be determined in a thing, in planning, in your preparation but once the plan is in place comes the need to determination in travel.

You can have all the maps and provisions in front of you, but a determined person will then use the maps and provisions because they are on that journey. Act!

SELF-BELIEF

Wow! It's easy to say, simple to spell and even easier to define. Self-belief is belief in oneself.

They say sport is a game of skill, luck, and confidence. We can do plenty about skill by training and listening to our coach. We can't do much about luck although some reckon the harder they train the luckier they get.

Show Up to RISE UP!

But what, if anything, can we do about confidence? Hang on. If we work hard at numbers one and two maybe, just maybe, number three will suddenly and magically appear.

With a strong belief in our own abilities, we tackle life with enthusiasm. We find our life is enjoying the snowball effect. You know, as the snowball rolls downhill it gets bigger and faster. Our success feeds off itself and we grow in confidence and speed.

BE RELENTLESS

Don't give up. If you have a goal, a product, or an idea that you really want to be successful, you have got to be relentless in your pursuit. Most of us do not realize that if we have something we really want to do, if it is considered our passion, and we want to excel, we may have to talk to a lot of people before we can find someone who will buy into our passion. So, ask yourself...Is your life moving up? Or is it moving down? No matter which direction it's going, you are in control. And if you want to begin to turn things around, it will require perseverance on your part.

YOU MUST NEVER GIVE UP!!!

Perseverance is an act of free will. We act on our

plan. Good luck often favors those who work hard at their goal. And because we take action and seek to improve our traveling, we grow in confidence and self-belief. It can be done.

"Self-confidence is the first requisite to great undertakings"

-**Samuel Johnson**

Show Up to Rise Up!

Taking Responsibility for Your Life

There is a Key to Finding Personal Happiness and it's called "Taking Responsibility"

CHAPTER 8

Dr. Madeline Ann Lewis

TAKE RESPONSIBILITY FOR YOUR LIFE

HERE IS A KEY TO FINDING personal happiness and it's called "taking responsibility." It's a simple situation. You plan your actions and whatever happens be it a good or not so good result, you are the one to blame or to take the credit.

Those who do take responsibility for their actions have a definite and measurable form of control over their life. People who are in control by virtue of hard work feel a sense of pride in being able to influence what happens.

One of the saddest scenes in life is the person who won't take responsibility for their life. "It's not my fault. This happened because someone or something let me down," is what they often say.

Now of course there are events which we can't control. An accident which is unavoidable is one example but there are so many things which we can control.

If we ignore good dietary advice and spend hours

stretched out on the sofa, we are not doing our health and weight any favors. Who is responsible for that? You are.

If we don't prepare well for an exam and get a low grade who is responsible for that? You are.

This is one occasion where the "I" or "me" in life is really relevant. Don't look at others or at circumstances. Look at yourself. What do I want to achieve? Where do I want to go? How will I get there? Well knowing that, the "I" steps up to the plate and takes responsibility for getting there. It's called "taking responsibility."

It's also called "growing up." When we were kids, we trusted out parents to take care of us, to feed, shelter and clothe us. But there comes a time when our parents give us our freedom. We can go out without them. We can drive the car, shop, and go on dates all on our own. We can find paid employment and spend or save our own money.

In all these actions we are in charge of what we do and don't do. We are responsible. So, seize the responsibility and take control of your own life.

DON'T BE AFRAID TO LEAD

Not all of us are suited to being an outstanding

public leader. It takes someone special to run a major corporation or even a local scout troop. But we can all be leaders when it comes to our own life. Every day we need to make decisions. Things like the time we get up, the food we eat, the way we choose to travel, the effort we put in at work or around the home and the amount of exercise and sleep we get.

In all these tasks decisions need to be made by you. You are the leader of your own life. You make the decisions, you plan the activities, you review the results, and you make whatever changes are required. They may not be public decisions, but they do exist, and you are the one who makes them. You are running the company.

So even the person who is the least likely to be a leader in society is still a leader in their own life. Of course, they could be a leader in other ways too like caring for a small child or elderly parents. Making decisions on their behalf also makes you a leader. You take responsibility for their health and well-being. You are in charge.

So, we are all leaders in one way or another. But then comes the question – what sort of leader are we? How do we rate as a leader?

If for one moment you view leadership as the

responsibility to keep others down or in one place, then I guarantee that your company, church, or community will not reach the goals it could or should. Either you are for growth or against it...and not just your own. The only way to lead is to practice leading. And part of being a good leader is learning how to win with humility and lose with dignity.

You've seen leaders in your job, at your church or sporting club and you see people as leaders in public life such as politicians and bosses. Some are brilliant and inspire others while some are okay and others you would rate with a really low score. But how do you rate yourself?

You can be a brilliant leader by taking sensible risks, by setting yourself goals and striving to achieve them and by rewarding yourself whenever you are successful.

TIPS ON BEING BETTER AT TAKING RESPONSIBILITY

- Become a person who completes a task. Finish what you start. Leaving a job half done doesn't help anyone especially you.

- Be punctual. Show up on time or even a little early.

- Listen to yourself, your inner voice. What you are thinking is what you may need to do.

- Listen to yourself, your outer voice. This means try and think about what you are saying, what people hear you say.

- Listen to others. Not everyone is wise, but most people have an idea or two which might just be right for you. If you receive criticism try and review it in a calm manner. Maybe there is some truth in the criticism and if that helps you improve, the criticism is worthwhile.

- Watch your body language. If you are positive and enthusiastic, your body language will show those feelings and that attitude.

- Think positive. Be optimistic; see the glass as half-full. With a positive outlook you will want to take responsibility and remember, those who do take responsibility for their own actions are more fulfilled and lead happier lives.

THE DO'S AND DON'TS OF HANDLING

SHOW UP TO RISE UP!

YOUR ANGER

We all get angry. It's a normal human emotion. The issue is in how we deal with our anger. Because women already are behind the eight ball with the general notion of being more emotional to begin with, you need to know how to keep your anger in check. There are times and ways to express anger.

DO

- Stay calm and control your voice.
- Take a deep breath.
- Communicate your feelings positively.
- Listen with an open mind.
- Stick to one issue at a time.

DON'T:

- Yell, cry, or accuse.
- Dig up old arguments or problems.
- Place blame.
- Point a finger or use any inappropriate body language.
- Think it's the end of the world.

Anger is a fact of life. Being effective means finding your way through conflict resolution.

DR. MADELINE ANN LEWIS

Model with phrases like: "In my opinion…," "The way I see it…," or "It seems to me…." Avoid being dominant, demanding, or demeaning. It is perfectly acceptable to display anger at the appropriate time. However, it must be calculated. Learn to control your emotions, to express your objections thoughtfully, and not in the heat of the moment.

"Action springs not from thought, but from a readiness for responsibility."

-Dietrich Bonhoeffer

SHOW UP TO RISE UP!

Stop Blaming Others

CHAPTER 9

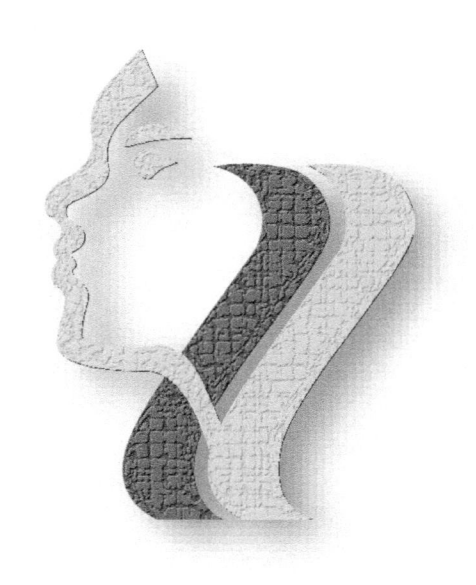

DR. MADELINE ANN LEWIS

STOP BLAMING OTHERS

TO GET THE BEST OUT OF YOURSELF there are many things you can add to your life. Punctuality, optimism, good health and fitness, positive attitude and love are just a few. But you will also make great progress if you can remove or get rid of some things. Those things are pretty much the opposite of the good things, Ditch lateness, negativity, obesity, and hate.

But there is another aspect of life which, once eliminated, will give your life a huge boost. Dump excuses.

Excuses are a real drag on your progress towards happiness and success. They slow your progress and even stop it; they narrow your vision, build complacency and stifle ambition. Dump excuses.

FAMOUS OR RATHER INFAMOUS EXCUSES

- The traffic was horrendous.
- I couldn't find my keys.
- The dog ate my homework.
- My alarm didn't go off.

Show Up to Rise Up!

- I thought it was next week.
- The cops pulled me over.
- The machine swallowed my card.
- The sky fell in.

SUCCESS EQUALS RESPONSIBILITY

We all want success. It might be a personal battle only you know about, or it could be a challenge the whole world knows about. But a major obstacle to you being successful is the making of excuses. If you make excuses, you fail.

When we talk about taking responsibility, a major part of that is not making excuses. If you are responsible for your own actions, you will not make excuses.

Excuses are a dead weight. Let's say you have a task and you begin work. You get closer to completion and there is pressure at home. You suddenly need a plumber, or the fridge breaks down. The simple course of action is to stop work on your task and use an excuse for your failure to complete the task on time.

Alternatively, if you refuse to deal in excuses, you will adapt. You will find a way around your domestic strife and better manage your time. You will work overtime to make up the time lost when you had to deal with your domestic crisis.

And what will happen if you refuse to make excuses? You'll complete your task which, because you did so despite the problems in-house, will make you feel doubly terrific. Success will be loitering with intent waiting to invade your inner being. You see you find your best inside when you perform your best outside.

EXCUSES ARE ALIVE

An excuse is a living being. It has a life of its own. It doesn't hide in the closet or behind the desk. It's fit and healthy and ready to spring into action. You need to know this. You need to know that excuses can stop you dead in your tracks. You need to be proactive and thus be ready when an excuse bounces into your life.

Have a program, a routine of not making excuses. If problems arise, work through them. Be flexible and adapt your schedule to still achieve your target. Ignore excuses. Avoid excuses. Shun excuses.

One useful tip is to spend your free time thinking positive thoughts. Think about the success you will have once you complete your task. By filling your mind with powerful thoughts of success, you

Show Up to Rise Up!

obliterate the negative thoughts as found in excuses. Overcome the negative by fixing your thinking on the positive.

"Ninety-nine per cent of all failures come from people who have the habit of making excuses."

-George Washington Carver

Find Your Authentic Voice

CHAPTER 10

SHOW UP TO RISE UP!

FIND YOUR AUTHENTIC VOICE

WE EACH HAVE OUR OWN PERSONALITY. We are all unique. Regardless of our status, wealth, or education, we are all an individual. And our personality is always on display. We show our personality through our language, our thoughts, and our actions. Our "voice" can refer to our whole person and not just the words we utter.

What we should, no must strive for continually is a genuine outpouring of our true self. Sadly, what some people see is not what they get. There are people who put up a facade or a false front. There are some people who are acting in real life.

This is wrong for several reasons.

- It does nothing for our self-esteem. We might be able to fool some others, but we sure can't fool ourselves.

- It causes people to treat us differently. They think we are a certain type of person and so respond accordingly. We should always seek to have others accept the real person.

DR. MADELINE ANN LEWIS

- Honesty is the best policy. By seeking to live to the highest ideals, we help ourselves and others. By cheating and pretending to be someone we are not, we let down so many people.

BE REAL

The opposite of course is to be a fake. Your job is to be yourself. If you find your best inside, if you do good in all ways, it will be easy to show the world the real you. You will be a perfect example of "what you see is what you get." Trickery eventually fools no-one, and it certainly won't fool you. Time and again we hear a parent, teacher, a coach or even a friend give good advice when they say, "Be yourself."

If your self-confidence needs a boost, there are ways of doing so. If your public-speaking skills need support, there are ways of gaining such skills. If your self-esteem is low, there are ways to change that situation for good. And if you improve your posture, position, and appearance, you are ideally placed to be natural.

LET YOUR INNER VOICE GUIDE YOU

Your inner voice is the whisper that gives you

motivation, inspiration, and hope in the mist of despair. Once you are aware that you have an inner voice, it becomes necessary to open your mind to the possibilities. Your inner voice is instinct, it does not hesitate, and your voice knows all of your possibilities. Go with your "gut" feeling. Do not doubt yourself. To find your passion in life, let your inner voice guide you. Go to bed with a question on your lips knowing that your answer will come. Your inner voice always has the best intentions for you if you will just tap into it and listen.

SHARE YOUR VOICE

When you allow your inner voice to guide you, your transformation is instantaneous. You now have a quiet knowing. Your body radiates internal strength and confidence. Your life is in sync and the people you need will naturally gravitate towards you. There is no room for ego, be kind, be generous and it will come back around to you. Share the knowledge of your inner voice because satisfaction like happiness is contagious.

Your voice then is the real thing.

HOW TO IMPROVE YOUR VOICE

There are several aspects of living you can work

on to improve your "voice."

- Become a good listener. Having good things to say is fine but being able to listen is as good and may even be better.

- Go deeper. So many people today look at and work on a shallow level. Don't be afraid to go deeper in your thinking, in your concern for others and in your planning to today and tomorrow.

- Become a whole person. We know about our physical life, which can involve our health and well-being but there are other aspects we should never neglect. Our mental health is vital. Our spiritual health too can be a great source of help. Setting aside time and keeping your spiritual health in order is important.

- Quiet times are good. We are so busy these days we seldom stop to contemplate. Make the time even if it's only a few minutes. Meditation takes many forms. Find one which works for you. Stop everything and contemplate your current position and your future.

Show Up to Rise Up!

- Indulge in the luxury of dreams. Thinking good thoughts about how you can be a better person pushes towards that style of behavior. Developing attributes of patience and determination will help make your dreams a reality.

- Improve your skills. We can always be better at what we do or begin a new skill and develop it. The challenge in obtaining the skill has many benefits and once the skill is mastered more benefits flow.

You'll give your "voice" a wonderful makeover by concentrating on the points above.

LIVE YOUR PASSION

It's a simple question. What do you care most about in your life? It could be you, your family, career, hobby, or faith. It could be more than one thing. But it all boils down to why you are here on Earth. What do you want to do with the rest of your life?

Again, this returns us to the destination and direction situation. If you know where you wish to go, if you know your destination, it is so much easier to make travel plans which will get you where you want to go.

DR. MADELINE ANN LEWIS

Here's the deal. Discover the purpose of your life and then set about fulfilling it. But don't just stroll through life. Put passion into the pursuit of your passion.

The first step is to make sure you have some purpose in your life. Some of the most unhappy people in life are those who go through the motions of their life day by day. We all need to reflect on our life. What do you want to achieve today, tomorrow and in ten year's time? And more importantly, what am I doing to make this happen?

We hear much about makeovers in the cosmetic surgery sense but what do we hear about people examining their inner lives? Are they happy? If not, why not?

There are cheap answers such as the need for more money, but real and lasting happiness comes from being at peace with yourself and the world. A person at peace is someone who knows what they want in life, has a plan to reach that goal and works hard to achieve it.

And if your goal is something which benefits your fellow human beings, you will double your sense of goodwill to others and, most of all, to yourself. One skill we can all consider is being able to

Show Up to Rise Up!

discover our purpose in life. It might be you are unsure and if so, how can you put passion into your goal in life if you are unsure of the goal in the first place?

Consider any number of ways to discover your purpose in life by attending one-on-one sessions with a therapist or by studying self-help books and DVDs designed to help you discover your purpose in life.

"Passion makes the world go round. Love just makes it a safer place."

-Ice T

Knowledge is Power.
Do You Have the Power?

CHAPTER 11

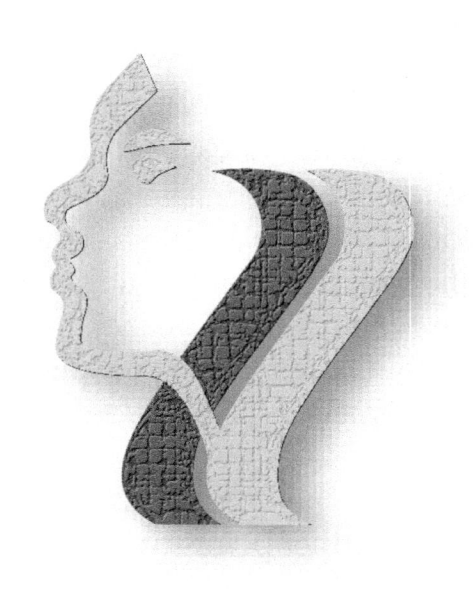

Show Up to RISE UP!

KNOWLEDGE IS POWER. DO YOU HAVE THE POWER?

ON THE SURFACE THAT SEEMS LIKE A SIMPLE STATEMENT. If you have knowledge, skills, and abilities, you are in a position to lead, create and be in demand. But the world is constantly changing and so the *knowledge is power* statement in 1600 does not have the same meaning today.

Here's an example. When Shakespeare was writing his plays, the English language had about 25,000 words. Today English has more than a million words. So once a person could know most if not all the words in their language and thus their knowledge would indeed make them powerful. Today most English-speaking people would know only a small fraction of the words in their own language.

And there are further points to consider regarding the *knowledge is power* statement.

- What type of knowledge gives power?

DR. MADELINE ANN LEWIS

- What type of power does knowledge provide?

- Has the statement always been true?

- Is it really true today?

Surely there is knowledge and there is knowledge. Someone who knows much about chemistry and the disease of the human mind is in a position to design medicines which might help the mentally ill. But someone who knows the names of all the left-handed batters who played Major League baseball in the 20th century is powerful in that .... well, how? Certainly, at trivia nights? Knowledge takes different forms.

So when we say that knowledge is power, we need to specify what we mean by knowledge because the type and nature of the knowledge may make a huge difference in providing power.

Then there's the reverse. If we gain power from having knowledge, what type of power do we gain? Is this power helpful to humankind? Is there a good and bad use of power? Well...the study of the history of war and the history of beneficial scientific discovery clearly illustrates the value of different types of power.

Show Up to RISE UP!

YESTERDAY AND TODAY

It's possible to argue effectively that *knowledge is power* has always been true but how powerful is something to discuss. In ancient times those who could read and write were certainly more powerful than the mass of illiterate people.

But how does this work today? Here are some examples of contemporary society where there is a compelling case supporting the statement that knowledge is power.

- Employment. Many jobs require certain qualifications. You might be a skilled operator but without that qualification you are not even in the hunt.

- Promotion. Within your trade you can move up the salary scale if you have additional qualifications.

- Self-employment. If you have knowledge in such things as web-page design, music recording, horticulture, jewelry manufacture or public speaking, you are well placed to become a powerful trader or performer.

HOW DOES THIS APPLY TO ME?

Dr. Madeline Ann Lewis

All the debates and discussions are fine, but this book is all about you the reader. And so, the question arises, do you have knowledge? Are you powerful? You see if it's true that knowledge is power and is certainly true today, where are you in the power stakes? Are you riding high, languishing in mediocrity, or failing badly?

There are two issues here.

1. You have a power ranking – good, bad, or indifferent and
2. You can change your ranking.

Look at your power ranking. What is the sum total of your knowledge? Remember it will include qualifications, skills, and expertise. List the types of knowledge you possess. This is List A. Describe each aspect. Let's say one type of knowledge you have is the ability to read, write and speak Italian. Is that a brilliant knowledge, an okay knowledge, or a very basic knowledge? The rankings will form List B.

So, you'll make two lists. List A states the type of knowledge and List B describes its condition.

TAKE CONTROL OF YOUR OWN DESTINY

Show Up to Rise Up!

Now comes the time to take action. It's easy because everything is in your own hands. Look at your lists. You have a choice here. You can choose to add to list A, which is the type of knowledge you already possess or from List B, you can improve or upgrade the level of expertise in some or all of your knowledge areas.

You could even do both.

But the point here is that **you are in charge**. You can alter your knowledge base. And if you add to your areas of knowledge and/or improve the quality of your knowledge, **you will become more powerful**.

It's as certain as night follows day. It's a join the dots to complete the picture situation. Improve your knowledge status and immediately acquire more power.

With your new or improved knowledge, you automatically become more powerful. And power in this case can benefit your life in many ways.

- You will feel happier inside. A sense of achievement in something worthwhile always does wonders for your self-esteem.

DR. MADELINE ANN LEWIS

- You will be in a stronger position to earn more money.

- You will attract more people to your words and actions.

- And your life will become more interesting.

These are exciting times. Not only because there is a surefire way of growing your inside and this growth brings multiple benefits but because you are in charge. You can control your own destiny.

"It's choice, not chance, that determines your destiny"

-Jean Nidetch

Show Up to RISE UP!

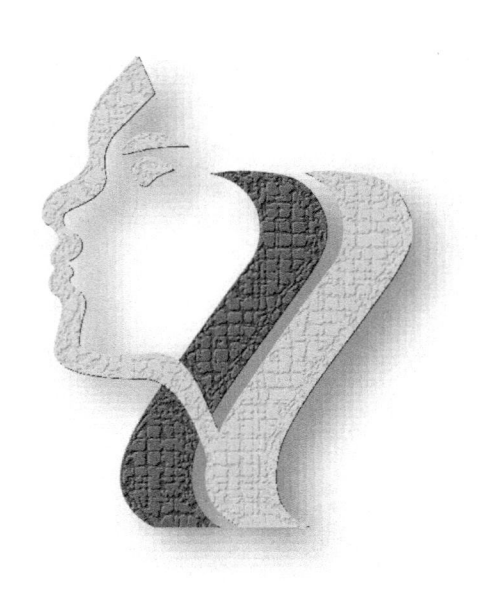

Those Shoes Are Made for Walking
But Not All Over You!
CHAPTER 12

DR. MADELINE ANN LEWIS

THOSE SHOES ARE MADE FOR WALKING: BUT NOT ALL OVER YOU!

LEE HAZELWOOD WROTE THE HIT SONG *THESE BOOTS ARE MADE FOR WALKIN'* IN 1965. It was huge. And one of the tests of the popularity of a hit song is if other artists later record the number. Many have and 40 years after Nancy Sinatra made it a hit, Jessica Simpson came along with another version including some new lyrics written by Simpson. In fact, there are literally over 200 different versions of the song.

Now what has all that musical history and the lyrics of the song got to do with self-improvement and taking control of your own destiny? Plenty. Let's look at some of the lessons we can learn from this musical example.

Copy success. If you have a blueprint which works, consider copying it. The original song was a hit and many cover versions were made. They too were successful. And time is not a factor. The Jessica Simpson version came along 40 years after the first recording.

Show Up to Rise Up!

So, if you meet or hear of someone who has a great life and work balance, who is happy in themselves and has control of their own destiny, surely you would want to check out their program. Why are they so successful and contented? What is their secret? We can always learn from others and copying what works for someone else might be the key to you finding happiness and success.

Words can have different meanings. In the Nancy Sinatra version, the lyrics were basically about a woman leaving her man. Jessica Simpson wrote new lyrics with her emphasis being on the individuality and growth of the women in the story.

When we look at words like *control, destiny, action,* and *happiness*, we need to ask how they are relevant to us. What one person regards as success may not be the same definition for another. You need to fine what you believe is your ideal position and having defined it, create a plan or timetable to achieve that position.

Take action. The lyrics are about doing something, about taking action. In the first version it's about boots [or shoes] not being there for decoration or protection but for helping the woman do something. In this case it's leaving an unhappy relationship but it's a definite type of action. This is what we should all consider. Once we figure out our destination in life, planning the direction is much simpler and clearer.

I said all that to say, many of you will never experience living your dreams because you are not willing to do what is required to make it happen. While I might sound a bit negative here, I am truly and deeply worried by what I sometimes see going on around me. There is a lot of talk about living our purpose, vision, and dreams. But not many people are putting the process of achievement into action. Most have become comfortable just reading and talking about dreams.

My goal here is to inspire you to make a move, take the first step. You can say to yourself or to others, the time is not right, the economy is not right, I have too many other things to do, but if you do that, there will never be a perfect time. So, step out on faith, make up your mind right now to get started and take action. If I could, I would sit beside you and help pull you away from all those burdens and responsibilities you are holding on to so tightly. But I can't, it must be your decision. There is no looking back now; it's full steam ahead.

You have shoes, you can walk, so use your legs.

SHOW UP TO RISE UP!

Make a plan and carry it out.

MIND HOW YOU GO

This is an expression in some places meaning *Take care* or *Be careful* or *Look after yourself*. It's an apt add-on to the order or admonishment to take action. By all means get moving but in doing so be careful that you don't damage yourself or others.

The problem for some people is that they fail to take action. They drift or lapse into mediocrity. This never works because anything worthwhile is only achieved by hard work and planning.

But if you do make plans and you do work hard you must ensure that the result is not damage to yourself or to others. Take some examples.

Too much too soon is the cause of many a problem. You decide you want to lose weight and draw up a program involving diet, exercise, and meditation. But by going too fast in too short a time you could finish up creating health problems which weren't there in the first place. Be active, even be pro-active and do so in a sensible and careful manner. You could even take advice from a professional.

Hurting others is not something you ever want to

do. But unfortunately, being determined to succeed in an area you could cause pain to those around you. It might be a friend, family member or work colleague. Be aware that your action is not harmful to others. In making plans to achieve your goal, consider how your action might impact on those around you.

> *"We should be taught not to wait for inspiration to start a thing. Action always generates inspiration. Inspiration seldom generate action."*
>
> -**Frank Tibolt**

Show Up to RISE UP!

Having A Coach.

CHAPTER 13

DR. MADELINE ANN LEWIS

HAVING A COACH.

ONCE UPON A TIME ONLY SPORTING TEAMS HAD A COACH. Now they exist in many spheres of life. Sporting teams of course still have a coach but now there are many. Assistants and specialists abound.

Then we have life coaches and career coaches. Mentors, personal trainers, and advisors are on call as well. What's this coaching business all about? Well, put simply it's a recognition of at least two things.

- It's a competitive world out there and

- We all need guidance to improve our abilities.

Life can bring us both highs and lows. What we need is an ability to handle the rough with the smooth. Anyone can shine when the weather is fine, but it takes skill, perseverance, and a strong character to do well when the weather is nasty.

That's where a life coach and career coach can be a huge plus. Let's consider some of the aspects of life, may be your life, in which a life coach or career coach can be an asset or even a life saver.

BENEFITS OF A LIFE COACH

Lacking direction? Are you a drifter? Do you have a plan for your life and are you able to stick to it? What we need is a good direction or purpose and then the skills and determination to follow that direction. A life coach can help you find and describe that direction and then help you on your journey towards that direction.

Perhaps you have a direction but find that time is your biggest enemy. In this case you need advice in time management. You need to discover how to get the best out of every day. A life coach can help you manage your time efficiently.

Moral support is often required. If you feel you are alone, perhaps only treading water in your life or are making progress but not receiving proper recognition, a life coach can give your confidence a boost and build your self-esteem stocks.

Are you a self-aware person? Are you able to successfully review your own behavior? Do you know which things in your life are holding you back? For an accurate assessment of your life, you need a life coach who can show you your weaknesses but better still, teach you how to analyze your own activities.

Ambition can be a two-edged sword. Too much and we fall back at being unable to reach our goals. Too little and we never discover our true potential. A life coach can help you develop the right balance in your ambition. You need enough ambition to challenge you and to take you out of your comfort zone.

WHY DO I NEED A CAREER COACH?

There are so many situations in which you need a career coach. Let's consider some of these situations. Do you see yourself in one or more of these cases?

What is important to you? You may have a career and it may even be successful but are you fulfilled? Making good money is not necessarily going to make you happy. You need to discover what things in life and your career are important to you. When you know this, you can adjust your goals and career accordingly. A career coach can help you learn which things are important to you.

How do you reach your chosen goals? You may

be in the career of your choice and have a plan of how you can win a promotion. But will you achieve your goals? Should you stay with your current employer or perhaps move elsewhere? What steps do you need to take to achieve your goals? A career coach can show you the steps and help in the planning of your task.

Are you passionate about your job? Are you going through the motions and finding little job-satisfaction? A career coach can turn around your mindset so that you become passionate about what you do for a living. As a result, your job-satisfaction levels soar and life itself becomes far more satisfying and rewarding.

Having a partner can give your career prospects a shot in the arm. Having a partner who knows about career management, inspiration and people skills means you are no longer alone in your career. A career coach can be an invaluable partner.

TEN BENEFITS OF HAVING A COACH

- You will get your work/life balance in order
- Your self-confidence and self-esteem will rise

- You will develop clear goals and a vision to achieve them

- You will be better at making deals

- Your people-handling skills will improve

- You will manage your time well and not the other way around

- You will be better at communication

- You will be better at solving problems

- Your networking skills will improve

- You will feel better inside

"Good coaches teach respect for the opposition, love of competition, the value of trying your best, and how to win and lose graciously."

-Brooks Clark

Show Up to RISE UP!

Don't Be Afraid to
Claim Your Blessings

CHAPTER 14

Dr. Madeline Ann Lewis

DON'T BE AFRAID TO CLAIM YOUR BLESSINGS

SOMETIMES OUR BIGGEST ENEMY IS OURSELF. Sometimes we hold ourselves back. Sometimes we fail to get the most out of ourselves because we lack compassion, we don't think big enough or worry that we don't fit in.

There can be many reasons why we never discover our best inside, why our grades are low, our career is stalled, or our personal happiness levels are down. We need to find these reasons and overturn them.

It's always sad when people fail to reach their true potential but it's doubly sad when the reason for this failure is not claiming our blessings.

There are many aspects to life which some of us ignore in part or in whole. For example, do you know how far you can progress in your career? Do you know how much self-fulfillment you can achieve? Have you claimed the gifts you are offered?

TRUE TO YOURSELF

Are you being true to yourself? Are you following your own conscience? Many people have a sense of right and wrong but choose not to live by these rules. This eats away at their self-esteem and pulls them back in terms of achieving their true potential. You know which path you should tread so not taking it prevents you from finding your best inside.

Why would you not accept certain gifts you are offered? It might be in your career or social life or in family relationships. You can be a kind and giving person and if you are, you will help those around you and certainly yourself. By choosing not to be kind or worse, to be cruel or unhelpful, you make life hard for others and harden your own heart.

If you have the skill to complete certain tasks and choose not to use your skills or choose not to improve your skills, your achievements don't occur or are weaker at best. Use your skills and improve the ones you have already. Make your output the best it can be and in so doing you benefit others and your self-esteem and self-confidence.

DR. MADELINE ANN LEWIS

Persistence is a wonderful virtue. So many people start out on a journey and then quit; some even within touching distance of the finish line. Train yourself to persist. Adopt a positive approach and be sure to carry on when times are tough. Only those who endure will attain their goal. And by persisting you develop great inner strength, and your character develops appreciably.

Be wary of worrying about what others think of you. We all want to be liked but the best judge of our character is yourself. We need to be proud of our own attitude and discipline. We should never set out to offend others, but fear of offending others can cause us to change our approach to life. Fix your goal and work diligently never worrying about how others may judge us.

Remove the dead wood. We all carry baggage. It might be a bad habit we've had for years or an attitude we've picked up in recent times; anything which stifles our growth or holds us back needs to be eliminated. Finding our best inside certainly means taking on positive attributes but it also means ditching bad ones. Analyze your behavior. The things which have a negative impact on your life should be dropped.

BLESSINGS ALREADY EXIST

Show Up to Rise Up!

One problem for some people is that they think they need to work extremely hard or pay some exorbitant price to obtain certain blessings. Nothing can be further from the truth.

Blessings such as the ability to forgive, to understand others and to love are freely available. It's just that some of us refuse to accept these gifts. We bear a grudge or practice a hatred of certain people or lock down our feelings. By releasing our inner thoughts and feelings and removing the anti-human perceptions, we make ourselves so much happier not to mention those around us. Take hold with a passion those gifts which are abundantly available to all of us.

"A true friend is the greatest of all blessings, and that which we take the least care to acquire."

Francois de La Rochefoucauld

In Conclusion

You Know the Expression, "LOOK In the Mirror" ...

CHAPTER 15

IN CONCLUSION: YOU KNOW THE EXPRESSION, "LOOK IN THE MIRROR"

YOU KNOW THE EXPRESSION, "LOOK IN THE MIRROR." This could apply to us all. It means that we give ourselves an examination, we examine our inner being, our thoughts, attitudes and desires. But it needs a certain type of examination. We need to adopt a critical approach to the looking.

A cursory glance in the mirror may not see the blemishes in our makeup, clothing, or hair. We need to make a serious effort.

Improving our life, discovering our best inner self and reaching our true potential can only occur when we know our current state of health. Are we healthy in the attitude stakes? We are not in a position to make the necessary changes if we have the wrong attitude and our unwillingness to truly discover our current inner health.

WHAT NEEDS TO BE DONE?

This book sets out to help us in a number of practical ways. By adopting the suggestions set out in this book we give ourselves a chance to make some serious and profound changes for the good. Here is a summary of those steps.

- What is your destination? It might be for today, tomorrow or for the rest of your life but you need a precise destination.

- What is your current direction? Will your current direction get you to your destination?

- Never blame others. Always accept full responsibility for your own actions.

- Forget limitations. "Aim high" is a great motto.

- You are unique. Don't try and be someone else. Find out who you are and star in your own life.

- Improve. You can always get better. Gain new skills or refine the ones you have.
- Take action. Planning anything means thinking but once the plan is in place, get moving.

- Be kind to others. Gaining something but hurting others is a false victory.

- You don't have to travel alone. Using a life and/or career coach could be one of the best moves you ever make.

Show Up to RISE UP!

- Make use of your blessings. We can all love, forgive and help others. Use these gifts to help others and make yourself a better person.

OVER TO YOU

Discovering your best inside is a process. It's a process we can all understand and see though to the finish. But it's also a never-ending process and one which helps us every day in so many ways. **Discover your best inside and then show up to rise.** Because in the end, when you do, everyone wins!

All truths are easy to understand once they are discovered; the point is to discover them.
Galileo

A FINAL WORD TO THE LADIES!!!
Get off the Treadmill of Life

Many of you talented, creative, and passionate women have stepped into the role of Superwoman. You have donned the cape and mask that have actually hindered your chances for a feeling of success and peace. Yet, because you chose to put on the Superwoman costume, you can just as easily choose to take it off. You have the potential and ability to become a woman with less stress and openness and simply do the best that you can do without the compulsive need to be perfect.

LADIES YOU NEED TO ASK YOURSELF:
Do I identify with the Superwoman Syndrome?

- Do I feel the need to do it all?
- Do I compete against myself?
- Do I rarely say "no" to others
- Do I take on more and more responsibility?
- Do I rarely feel a strong sense of accomplishment
- Do I constantly feel overwhelmed?
- Do I feel the need to be the perfect mother/wife/daughter?
- Do I want to be everything to everyone?

Here are a couple of tips that will help you have a more fulfilling life:

KEEP LIFE SIMPLE!!!

Begin leading a simpler and less chaotic life by starting with a life mission statement. In this mission statement, make a list of survival roles, or actions and behavior to get you through day by day. Next, write down everything that is vital to obtaining prescribed lifetime goals.

Finally, list areas of your life that you feel do not

SHOW UP TO RISE UP!

need to be done or can be let go. Then when this is done, begin a new game plan. Write this plan as if for a best friend. Watch for time wasters. Learn to say "no" often and without guilt. Reward new behavior. Live with the "needs" and do not complicate life with the "wants."

PAY ATTENTION TO EACH DAY!!!

First, get up earlier to allow some quiet, private time before leaving for work. Spend some time looking or going outside. What kind of day is it? What types of clouds are in the sky? Are there special sounds? Learn to pay attention to the "now"...do not be a "clock watcher." Regulate the number of items on your "to do" list. During lunch, avoid talking business, eat slowly and take a full hour. Go to lunch with an enthusiastic staff member. Make a list of "hyper habits" that include too much rushing around. Share this list with a friend and make a contract to alter some of these conflicting behaviors and to slow down.

Find a specific area near work, such as a park, where it is possible to go alone for some quiet time. Post written reminders at home on the mirror that state, "Today, I am going to be in a good mood." Be willing to say "no" when necessary. Ask for help when needed and delegate whenever it will be an advantage.

DR. MADELINE ANN LEWIS

Finally, before falling asleep, give thanks for one small or large success that occurred that day. Keep everything as simple as humanly possible.

There are so many benefits that will come from stepping off the treadmill and enjoying life without having to do it all. You need to throw away your Superwomen costume and keep life simple with a daily "no" and more concern for your own well-being. Be willing to get out of the boat of safety and move toward your destiny.

This is how you will begin to *Show Up to Rise Up*!!!

Blessings beyond and much success on all your future endeavors.

Dr. Madeline Ann Lewis
President/CEO
Executive Women's Success Institute &
Deline Lifestyle Travel Membership

To find out more about what Dr. Lewis, Executive Women's Success Institute and the Deline Lifestyle Travel Membership

Visit the official website: www.exwsi.com or Email: info@exwsi.com

Show Up to RISE UP!

Ladies

THIS IS THE MESSAGE OF MY LIFE....SHOW UP to RISE UP!

DR. MADELINE ANN LEWIS

A Word to the Ladies

A Personal Note

For most of us, life offers abundant opportunities for joy, pain, laughter, and tears. The good times you savor. The great times you treasure, and the hard times are part of the character of your heart and soul. Our ability to handle life challenges is a measure of our heart, faith, and character, but where do we learn how to deal with challenges, hard times, and difficulties? In school, it's the basics…reading, writing, arithmetic. But what about Life 101 - the keys to living? What about failed relationships, losing your job or a loved one? Those lessons are, unfortunately, acquired through the school of hard knocks. But oh, ladies and gentlemen, there are options for life when you make the decision to show up to rise.

This is the message of my life….to *Show Up to Rise Up*. Take the bookends of action that have framed my success--Abundance and Perseverance—and make the translation to the greatness that lies within you. No matter how difficult your life may become, no matter how hard life gets, there is always a reason to find your best inside so you can

Show Up to RISE UP!

show up to rise up. There is purpose to keep going with the evidence of abundance, and the perseverance to survive and thrive. Thrive, not just survive. Yes, I said thrive, not just survive.

As I share my journey, you will find yourself in one of three places.... celebrating, activating, and DEFINITELY persevering to your best inside. I can say this because every day we get the opportunity to grow – not just exist but to grow. Recognizing the heritage of your own divinity and power in the space of your daily life is where we all learn to acknowledge fear and adversity and hold on to its instruction only for the unique lesson that is yours.

You see acknowledgement creates the opening for adjustments. And if you can stay in control, adjustments generate resolutions, and resolutions are building blocks of a foundation of a life not riddled with fear. So, ask yourself right now: *Do you feel like you are failing your ABCs as an adult? Are your dreams more real than your fears? Are you finding comfort and if so, how is it entering your life? Is your mind creating the space of..." I am"?*

You must understand your mind is a powerful force, a creative force. Every time you say **"I am"** you are creating a positive reality. **"I am"** can be the two most powerful words in your thoughts, articulated in your vocabulary, even if you are not quite there yet. One of the most powerful mantras out there which could change your entire life is, *"I am receiving all good things right now with appreciation."* When you do this, you place an order in the Universe. You are affirming in the positive and in the present that which is your divine birthright:

Happiness...And what is better, you are automatically doing it from the position of gratitude. Of all the research done out there on positive thinking and attracting goodness in your life, maintaining an attitude of gratitude is the most crucial ingredient to seeing the good you want to manifest itself and begin to happen. Sometimes life is like a scratchy CD – It keeps repeating!!!

We live in very challenging times, stress at work, pressure in the workplace, with downsizing, rightsizing, and politics. People are constantly seeking to make sense of their lives. How do you keep going when the hard knocks of life don't seem to stop? It's one thing to be positive when things are going well, but it's altogether different when you are blind-sided or when things are just plain going wrong. Such as:

- When a loved one is taken away

SHOW UP TO RISE UP!

- When an illness strikes you or your family member
- When the basement floods or the hot water heater explodes, and everything seems "lost"
- When the relationship or friendship that has kept you going falls apart
- When you go through the emotional torment of a divorce
- When your grown children return home
- When a business partner betrays you
- When your teenagers seem more like adults

Any of these situations is enough to just make you scream..." GIVE ME A BREAK." Just give me a chance to catch my breath. But life does not always listen, but if you can navigate your course, the scream isn't about 'WHY.' When you know the best inside of you, the tune of the song is on the title track – *"I Am Glad to Have Another Chance."*

Winston Churchill once said: "Never Give Up. Never Give In. Be fearless when it comes to your own possibility because its not over until you.... *Show Up to Rise Up.* And when you find it by asking, believing, and receiving, get ready to design your own song.

You see...each of us has a choice to let hard times and fears dominate us, free us to the next level, OR we can get trapped and allow ourselves to see them as temporary setbacks. I write my books, my articles, I and speak because I want those of you who hear my words to discover your own exits of the highway of daily adversity. Every day you must eradicate negative thoughts before they take root, shape, or form in any way. Do not allow yourself to take the path of despair. Turn the ship around before you hit the glacier and sink like the Titanic.

So many of us are familiar with slippery ice on the path of life because we have traveled it before. Find the courage to try something new. It's your choice. Remember that "I am" is as powerful of a creative force in your life as "I am not."

YOU REALLY ARE WHAT YOU THINK YOU ARE! How can you understand the philosophy of Asking, Believing, and Receiving?

Ask… What I mean by ask is to first vocalize it! Put words to it. In the old days this was called casting a spell and for good reason. But the Bible tells us, "We have not, because we ask not." Words are so powerful; they are the first step in creating magic. Writing things down helps you get clear. Sometimes, you must let the stream of consciousness flow. Don't edit. The trick is to open the door and see what comes flooding out. There is no better way than writing to do this.

Show Up to Rise Up!

Why not keep your own journal of abundance? The record of your words is to see all the things which manifested because of you writing them down and it also helps to go back and read them as needed throughout your day. If you want to text yourself, do that too! Or use the fancy voice features on your phone to capture the thought. It doesn't matter the medium you use (including a bathroom mirror reminder if you need it). What matters is that YOU hold yourself accountable by asking yourself and keeping the thought in a single place. How do you begin your requests in life?

Bob Proctor, longtime teacher of the *Law of Attraction* suggests beginning each request with, I am so happy and grateful now that...and continuing your wish in the present tense as if you already have it, which leads us to the second point:

Believing...It is not enough to ask. You have got to believe your dreams are worthy, no matter what. The Universe is mysterious and abundant. The biggest problem to achieving your dreams happens when you have a deficit mentality, when you believe you must —rob Peter to pay Paul so to speak.

Abundance is not just the birthright of the rich or powerful. Abundance is the birthright of every living person. Many get stuck trying to make things happen or pushing to make it happen. I am not suggesting that you don't need to work hard to achieve your goals because you certainly do. More importantly, you must believe that your goals and your results are worthy of you. Feel good about yourself NOW! You are unique in the entire world to move, to take the next turn of your life, and receive.

Receive…Once you feel good, once you feel like you already have it (take an acting class if you need a jumpstart on dusting off your imagination) get ready to enjoy what is meant to be yours. In fact, get plain old excited about your "it" that you have asked for and believed in….is on its way. Receive it and be grateful, for you deserve all good things. Proof will be all around.

I like to think of the big "Z" the hero Zorro would leave after a huge rescue or coup. Done with

SHOW UP TO RISE UP!

panache and flair, sometimes even bursting in flames, we, the audience, are left with his lasting impression. So too, should you have a signature which tells the world you have left your mark. We can't all be Zorro, but each of us has a superhero inside of us which can be expressed more easily than you may think.

An ancient Roman senator once said, "In great attempts it is glorious even to fail." Now it may not have felt good at the time, you may have gone down that road of self-loathing, but look at it again: what did you see as a result of leaving that bad marriage only to discover love for yourself, or getting fired only to find something else come up like a better job, a call into a different profession entirely where you were better suited, the opportunity to begin anew and find balance that you can easily identify. This allows you to know your center when others may not, and to recognize when it may be going a drift. You are operating with a powerful navigator – the gifts that lie inside of you.

Will you encounter hard times? No doubt storms will rise, puddles may even help skid you off the path temporarily because everyone falls on hard times, challenges, and suffering. But if you give your endeavors the best you can and suffer when you let it go, do you realize what that pain symbolizes? It is a sign you lived or loved so courageously that tragedy entered your story, but it did not stay. Tragedy is very often the mark of a good life, not a ruined one. Up from the ashes, like the phoenix bird, the spirit rises, rises with the awareness of who you truly are.

Les Brown says, "Shoot for the moon. Even if you miss, you'll still be among the stars." The best way to get through these times of hardship is to look around you and notice other survivors. Look to the successful and find inspiration in them, they can always lend a helping hand. Remember evil works through the feeling of being isolated so connect, connect, connect.

The person that helped me to find my best inside and to show up to rise up was my mother. She was a woman of strength and character, a person who never gave up or used the word "can't." She instilled in me that I was special and that there was no limit to what I could accomplish if I believed in myself and never gave up on my dreams. She used to say, "at the end of the day be proud of what you have accomplished rather than being frustrated at what you did not do." She was a firm believer that you should always share your knowledge with those who need help or guidance. She also believed that when you get to the top you should pull someone up with you. These are the reasons

Show Up to Rise Up!

why I do what I do and why I'm passionate about helping women advance and excel in their personal and professional lives. Her words just seem to make sense to me.

As I began to understand my environment and how it propelled me forward, I also realized joining the military helped to reinforce what my mother taught me. The discipline and teamwork showed me that you stick with it until the end, no matter what. As I stood on the war lines of Dessert Storm where adrenaline of our entire troops ran to the edge of engagement, it was clear the need to move in unison and to stand down at a moment's notice to preserve peace. Yet, you could feel the still in the air – there was a higher sense of responsibility to help your fellow soldier. It was an act of decision-making that reminded me of the similarities of what my Mom taught me.

Life is a delicate balance of opportunity and decisions. And at the end of the day, you must be proud of what you did in that day. I learned from my Mom how to "find my best inside"; how to share knowledge and help others and to never give up; and how to show up to rise. And from the Army I learned how to adapt, improvise, and overcome in any situation and that teamwork was the best way to be successful in any mission.

Dr. Madeline Ann Lewis

Every event in your life, every person you encounter contributes to who you are, and who you are becoming. There is fluidity to your story, a score underlying the music of your dance. Taking time to chart and acknowledge this powerful inner journey is an incredible exercise. Try writing your autobiography. I don't mean you have to write a novel, but again, sit down and let the part of you that wants to be heard, acknowledged, and remembered flow onto the page. Be a reporter of other's stories and perhaps you can find your own. You will be surprised how many accomplishments you have under your belt, how many times you made a difference and how even your failures became a cornerstone of your success.

So now my question is…. what is the best inside of you? When do you feel would be the right time to share that with all of us? We are waiting for your signature. Alice Lutz, Founder of Oxygen Network once said, "It's not about "finding yourself" it's about designing yourself.

Designing yourself is about knowing the best inside of you. When you know you, it's like each day is its own birthday celebration. It's your birthday. It's your world of understanding and a code you live by because you can. Your dream won't deplete or steal from anyone else. There is

SHOW UP TO RISE UP!

an infinite, unending potential for all of us. There is endless possibility because YOU ARE YOU. Repeat it often...there is endless possibility because I am ME. There is endless possibility because I am ME. There is endless possibility because I am ME. If you conceive it, you can believe it and receive it.

I am Dr. Madeline Ann Lewis helping women to not only *find their best inside, but also to SHOW UP TO RISE UP, tap into their full potential, and conquer the world*. That's my signature, and I autograph it with grace and goodness.

Remember, it's not over until you find your best inside, and I want to see your autograph. So now is the time for you to **SHOW UP TO RISE UP!**

Blessings beyond!!!

ABOUT THE AUTHOR

DR. MADELINE ANN LEWIS

President/CEO of the Executive Women's Success Institute, International TEDx Speaker, International Bestselling Author, and creator of the online course *"Crack The Career Code: Unlock The Amazing Power Within To Lead With Confidence, Charisma, and Credibility."*

She's a retired Army veteran, the host of the *Success 4 Women Radio/TV Show,* Career Strategist, Trainer, Speaker, and Business Consultant.

Dr. Lewis conducts professional development training, workshops and seminars that have been presented throughout the United States and abroad. She received the

Show Up to Rise Up!

2024 Presidential Lifetime Achievement Award; the Acquisition International 2024 "Business Excellence Award"; the Prince George's Chamber of Commerce 2023 Excellence in Business "Visionary of The Year" Award; She also received the Most Influential Women Empowerment Coach Award, from Canadian Ambassador Her Excellency Denisa Gokovi; the Joe Manns Black Wall Street 2022 Award; the 2022 Veteran Champions of the Year (VCOY)" in Corporate America" list. The VCOY Corporate list honors 30 champions who advocate for our nation's veterans in the civilian workforce.

She received the Acquisition International 2022 "Most Empowering Women's Success Coach" Award; the 2017 Enterprising "Woman of the Year"; the Paul Anthony Foundation for the 2015 Successful Journey of Black Entrepreneurship" Award; she was chosen from hundreds of nominees around the world to receive Honorable Mention as a finalist for the "2015 Enterprising Woman of the Year" Award; she received the a "Certificate of Special Congressional Recognition" from Congresswoman Donna F. Edwards, for her participation in the 2014 Veterans History Project; she received the 2013 Prince George's Chamber of Commerce "Business Woman of the Year" Award; she also received a "Certificate of Congressional Recognition" from Congressman Steny H. Hoyer, because of demonstrated marked success in carrying out the mission of the Prince George's Chamber of Commerce; she was selected by the 2012 Minority Enterprise Executive Council for the "50 Women of Power in Business" Award; which is just a few of many accolades she has received.

Dr. Lewis has been featured and been quoted in numerous magazines, newspapers, on website front pages such as

DR. MADELINE ANN LEWIS

AOL.com and Yahoo.com and radio shows. She has written numerous articles that have appeared in business journals, online magazines, womenworking.com, federal magazines, and college websites.

Dr. Lewis served as Chair of the Woman's Advantage Forum a 12-month curriculum-based program (picked up by the Prince George's Community College Entrepreneurial Development Center), that helped women entrepreneurs grow their businesses to 6 & 7-figure revenue. She has been featured in the Woman's Advantage Wisdom Calendar four years in a row. She currently serves as the Board Director on the Sisters 4 Sisters Network, Inc.; She served as Board Director on the Justice Federal Credit Union for three years; on the Daughters of Zion Empowerment Center (a non-profit organization). She is on the International Advisory Board of the Professional

Woman Network, and she served as an Advisor for the Leadership Training Center located in Lanham, MD.
She is the author of *"Playing from the Blue Tee: Women in the Federal Government"* and *"Finding Your Best Inside: How to Persevere and Become the Person You Are Meant to Be."* She's also co-authored five other empowerment books.

HER MISSION IS TO
"Help Women Accelerate Their Path to Success."

PERSONAL QUOTE:
"Being proud of your background and unique attributes will ensure continued growth. Recognition provides the opportunity to speak about and showcase our experiences as women exhibiting strength in the business world."

SHOW UP TO RISE UP!

DR. MADELINE ANN LEWIS

153 | YOUR MINDSET IS YOUR SUPERPOWER OWN IT AND SOAR!

Made in the USA
Middletown, DE
15 November 2024